D'LISH

DEVILED

EGGS

CHIPOTLE
page 127

D'LISH

DEVILED

EGGS

A COLLECTION *of* RECIPES
from CREATIVE *to* CLASSIC
BY KATHY CASEY

photographs by KATHY CASEY FOOD STUDIOS
and DARREN EMMENS

**Andrews McMeel
Publishing, LLC**
Kansas City • Sydney • London

Andrews McMeel Publishing, LLC
an Andrews McMeel Universal company
1130 Walnut Street, Kansas City, Missouri 64106

www.andrewsmcmeel.com

www.kathycasey.com

13 14 15 16 17 SDB 10 9 8 7 6 5 4 3 2 1

ISBN: 978-1-4494-2750-4

Library of Congress Control Number: 2012947364

Edited by Jessica Duncan and Ann Manly
Food styling by Kathy Casey Food Studios
Designed by Alicia Nammacher and Kathy Casey Food Studios
Typesetting by Jessica Duncan

ATTENTION: SCHOOLS AND BUSINESSES
Andrews McMeel books are available at quantity discounts with bulk purchase
for educational, business, or sales promotional use. For information, please
e-mail the Andrews McMeel Publishing Special Sales Department:
specialsales@amuniversal.com

I WOULD LIKE TO DEDICATE THIS BOOK
TO ALL COOKS WHO GATHER FRIENDS
AND FAMILY AROUND THEIR TABLES AND
SURROUND THEM WITH *good food*.

CONTENTS

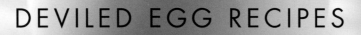

DEVILED EGG RECIPES

BOURSIN & GARLIC
WITH HERB SALAD
page 93

ACKNOWLEDGMENTS

In cooking it's not just one "thing" that makes an outstanding dish or meal. In the same way, a cookbook cannot be created alone, but takes the teamwork and dedication of a great crew.

I would like to thank my editor, Jean Lucas at Andrews McMeel, for believing that deviled eggs deserve their own book.

A grand D'Lish thank you to Jessica Duncan, who worked hand in hand with me on this book from inception to print, and everything in between.

Hats off to my wonderful team at the Food Studios for their creative brainstorming on all things deviled eggs, and for being consummate taste testers: Heather Jones, Erwin C. Santiago, Jason Anderson, and Cameo McRoberts. To longtime associate Ann Manly for her keen editing eye, my admiration and appreciation. As always, thank you to John Casey, my willing partner in all my culinary adventures.

My deepest thanks to those who made the pages of this book come alive: über-talented designer Alicia Nammacher, for bringing together the hard work and talents of everyone so beautifully and stylishly, and photographer Darren Emmens, for patiently coaching the Food Studios shots, and for his stunning photography work.

Last but not least, thank you to Chicky, our Food Studios mascot, for inspiring us to put the egg before the chicken and always making us smile . . . even when we had deviled eggs coming out of our ears.

INTRODUCTION

TWO-BITE
"CARBONARA"
DEVILED DUCK EGGS
page 112

❖ Deviled eggs have long been America's favorite appetizer; whether at a family reunion, holiday celebration, or cocktail party, they are usually the first thing to fly off the table.

❖ I first started getting creative with deviled eggs by experimenting with sassy chipotle eggs that had a fresh tomato and cilantro topping—they were a party hit! Next, it was on to Asian-inspired Thai curry eggs with a garnish of shrimp, cucumber, and fresh mint; then came cocktail hour with Bloody Mary–inspired stuffed eggs. After that, the sky was the limit!

❖ It was really fun coming up with the different recipes in this book; we brainstormed on appetizers, sandwiches, salads—could they be turned into a deviled egg? You bet! We also laid out ingredients that we thought were interesting and tasty, and incorporated them into new flavor concepts. Inspiration came from everywhere: travels, people, memories, new dishes, and old favorites.

❖ This book has a recipe for everyone and every occasion. For a taste of tradition, whip up a batch of Classic Picnic-Style (page 36) and Grandma's Old-Fashioned Deviled Eggs (page 39). Tried-and-true apps get a devilish makeover; in the "California Roll" Deviled Eggs (page 85), we took apart the sushi roll and made it into a deviled egg! It has all the essentials—avocado, wasabi, crab, pickled ginger, and tobiko. We even sprinkled on a little seaweed seasoning. Or get imaginative with new seasonings and ingredients, and try your hand at Tahini & Tabbouleh Deviled Eggs (page 108) or Fennel, Orange & Harissa Deviled Eggs (page 111). There are even recipes with a sassy spin on breakfast, such as French Toast Deviled Eggs (page 75) and Brunchy Deviled "Eggs Benedict" (page 77). With this many ways to dress up your next batch of stuffed eggs, they'll never go out of fashion.

❖ Flip through the pages for everything you need to know about perfect hard-cooked eggs, flavorful fillings, and piping tips. There's also a chapter with recipe suggestions for delightful party and holiday pairings so you're sure to be serving up the season's most stylish deviled eggs. After all, showing up at a party with a batch of deviled eggs will always get you invited back. So get cracking and cook up some D'Lish Deviled Eggs. —*Kathy*

GRANDMA'S
OLD-FASHIONED
page 39

DEVILED EGGS

PAST *and* PRESENT

❖ Deviled eggs might seem like a modern creation, thought up by some clever hostess looking for a classy handheld appetizer, but their history goes much further back. Aside from the generations-old family disclaimer that "Grandma So-and-So created this recipe . . ." (every family seems to have one!), the story of deviled eggs is somewhat foggy. It seems that no one really knows where they originated or who came up with the grand idea to stuff an egg with delicious ingredients. What we do know is that stuffed eggs have been around in various forms for centuries. That's right, the ancient Romans and Egyptians were eating stuffed eggs ever since fowl were first domesticated sometime around 6,000 BC!

❖ Apicius, the world's first known cookbook author, tells of eggs stuffed with pine nuts, lovage, pepper, and honey. According to cookbooks throughout history, boiling eggs, seasoning the yolks with various other ingredients, then restuffing them was a common practice, one that has been carried through modern times to become the beloved deviled egg as we know it.

❖ The name deviled eggs, however, is a product of eighteenth-century England. Deviled, as a culinary term, first appeared in text in 1786, to refer to foods that were highly seasoned and spicy. The connotation, unsurprisingly, came from the idea that the food was as hot as the Devil's hometown.

DEVILED EGG DISHWARE

"CALIFORNIA ROLL"
page 85

❧ Deviled-egg plates began taking hold as distinct servingware pieces early in the last century. Some of the first examples date to 1925 and were generally made of glass. It is believed that deviled-egg plates took after oyster platters, simply with smaller indentations. Makers of dinnerware sets quickly included the unique platters and they became a popular addition to a household's "good" china. In later years, egg plates appeared in a wider variety of materials, including pottery, metal, and even wood. Designs became more varied and featured decorations such as chickens and eggs—some are even shaped like them! Glass styles remained popular, though; hobnail-pattern platters in beautiful colors are among the most sought-after types.

❧ These days, thrifting and all things retro are chic again, bringing about a resurgence in the popularity of deviled-egg plates. I first saw them at tag sales, garage sales, and thrift stores—barely a dime a dozen then—and I started to become obsessed! Now you can find vintage specimens on eBay and Etsy, and it's a total score if you come across one at an estate sale or antique market. Prefer brand new? Today's specialty kitchen shops offer a variety of modern designs—even a porcelain one shaped like an egg carton that lets you serve deviled eggs done "up." Over the years, I've collected a cool selection of plates. One is edged in baby-chick-yellow ribbons, with tiny chicken salt and pepper shakers that nest in the middle. A friend brought back a sleek and sexy, oval silver dish from Mexico as a gift for me, and I even have one made of elegant cut crystal. Then there are the milk glass and lustrous carnival glass plates . . . can you ever really have too many?

❧ Not merely decorative—although they certainly can enhance your party theme, these specialized serving pieces are very useful for transporting deviled eggs. (If you do so often, consider a Tupperware version with lid and handle.) Having at least one simple, classic deviled-egg plate will ensure that your eggs always arrive in style, whether it's at a potluck or a cocktail party. After all, nothing is more disappointing than a wobbly plate of eggs sliding to and fro after you've spent all that time making them look perfect!

LUXE TRUFFLE
page 119

EGG-CEPTIONAL IDEAS

FOR HOLIDAYS *and* SPECIAL EVENTS

HOLIDAYS

Every day is a good day for deviled eggs! Here's a list of holidays, along with suggested recipes to liven up any appetizer spread. With a different food holiday every day, there's always an excuse to make a batch of deviled eggs and share them with a few food-loving friends. And don't forget, May is Egg Month—be sure to celebrate with lots of D'Lish Deviled Eggs!

♣ JANUARY 1 **NEW YEAR'S DAY:** Start off the new year with Bloody Mary Deviled Eggs, 79.

♣ **CHINESE NEW YEAR:** Based on a lunisolar calendar, the annual date of this holiday varies from January 21 to February 20. Chase out the old year and welcome a fresh start and good fortune with Firecracker BBQ Pork Deviled Eggs, 60, Wasabi Deviled Eggs, 90, or Ginger Chili Deviled Eggs, 89.

♣ FEBRUARY 14 **VALENTINE'S DAY:** Beet'ing Heart Deviled Eggs, 125, are a romantic shade of pink for your valentine. Sunny Roasted Red Pepper Deviled Eggs, 135, also blush for the day.

♣ MARCH 17 **SAINT PATRICK'S DAY:** Bring on the luck of the Irish with Devilish Green Eggs & Ham, 86, Green Goddess Deviled Eggs, 71, or Wasabi Deviled Eggs, 90. For a bit of tradition, whip up a batch of Corned Beef & Sauerkraut Deviled Eggs, 62.

♣ **EASTER:** This spring holiday brings us lots of decorated eggs, so what better time to make deviled eggs! Radishes & Butter Deviled Eggs, 133, and Emerald Asparagus & Sweet Onion Deviled Eggs, 122, celebrate the season's bounty. Green Goddess Deviled Eggs, 71, and Beet'ing Heart Deviled Eggs, 125, are especially colorful.

♣ APRIL 16 **EGGS BENEDICT DAY:** Brunchy Deviled "Eggs Benedict," 77, of course!

♣ APRIL 26 **PRETZEL DAY:** Honey Mustard Deviled Eggs, 101—they're topped with crushed pretzels!

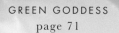

GREEN GODDESS
page 71

❖ MAY 5 **CINCO DE MAYO:** Add a little fiesta to your eggs with Chilaquile Deviled Eggs, 105, Southwest Salsa Deviled Eggs, 48, or Chipotle Deviled Eggs, 127.

❖ **MOTHER'S DAY:** Say thanks to Mom with a batch of Green Goddess Deviled Eggs, 71, or Boursin & Garlic Deviled Eggs with Herb Salad , 93. French Toast Deviled Eggs, 75, could be the star of breakfast in bed paired with a glass of bubbly.

❖ JUNE 19 **DRY MARTINI DAY:** Dirty Martini Deviled Eggs, 80.

❖ **FATHER'S DAY:** Show Dad he's #1 and serve up Steak & Deviled Eggs, 65, as a robust starter to a special dinner.

❖ JULY 4 **INDEPENDENCE DAY:** Bring the All-American Potato Salad Deviled Eggs, 68, or Grandma's Old-Fashioned Deviled Eggs, 39, to a picnic near you!

SOUTHWEST SALSA
page 48

❖ **LABOR DAY:** Wrap up the summer with Pimiento Cheese Deviled Eggs, 104, or Tahini & Tabbouleh Deviled Eggs, 108.

❖ OCTOBER 11 **WORLD EGG DAY:** Go international with Indian Curry Deviled Eggs, 107, Tahini & Tabbouleh Deviled Eggs, 108, Glorious Greek Deviled Eggs, 59, or Southwest Salsa Deviled Eggs, 48.

❖ OCTOBER 31 **HALLOWEEN:** Every ghost and ghoul at the party will love the "rotten eggs" a.k.a. Tapenade Deviled Eggs, 56.

❖ NOVEMBER 2 **DEVILED EGG DAY:** The best holiday of all! Throw a deviled-egg party and have everyone bring their favorite.

❖ **THANKSGIVING DAY:** Deviled Eggs Duxelles, 120, complements any holiday menu. When everyone else brings pie, surprise them with a "Pumpkin Pie" Deviled Eggs, 136, appetizer!

❖ **HANUKKAH:** Add deviled eggs to your celebration of the Festival of Lights with Smoked Salmon Deviled Eggs with Sour Cream & Chives, 47, or Goat Cheese & Peppadew Deviled Eggs, 67. Honey Mustard Deviled Eggs, 101, are topped with crunchy crushed pretzels.

❖ **CHRISTMAS:** Sunny Roasted Red Pepper Deviled Eggs, 135, Goat Cheese & Peppadew Deviled Eggs, 67, Wasabi Deviled Eggs, 90, and Devilish Green Eggs & Ham, 86, all display the emblematic red and green colors of the season. "Pumpkin Pie" Deviled Eggs, 136, are a festive twist.

❖ **KWANZAA:** For your family's Kwanzaa feast (Karamu), consider the sesame goodness of Tahini & Tabbouleh Deviled Eggs, 108, and celebrate with harvest Buttered Corn Deviled Eggs, 72.

❖ DECEMBER 31 **NEW YEAR'S:** Ring in the New Year with Lobster Deviled Eggs, 116, Luxe Truffle Deviled Eggs, 119, or Deviled Quail Eggs & Caviar, 115, made extra-special with a dusting of edible gold flakes!

PARTY IDEAS

Theme parties or just a gathering of friends are always occasions to celebrate. Here are some party ideas with suggested deviled eggs:

COCKTAIL PARTY

Deviled eggs are a natural pairing with cocktails:
Caesar Salad Deviled Eggs, 130
Bloody Mary Deviled Eggs, 79
"California Roll" Deviled Eggs, 85
Firecracker BBQ Pork Deviled Eggs, 60
Luxe Truffle Deviled Eggs, 119

"MAD MEN" THEME PARTY

Dish up some midcentury nostalgia:
Dirty Martini Deviled Eggs, 80
Old-School Onion Dip Deviled Eggs, 102
Retro Shrimp Cocktail Deviled Eggs, 82
20th Century–Style Deviled Eggs, 43

DINNER PARTY WITH FRIENDS

Serve a whimsical deviled-egg sampler:
Two-Bite "Carbonara" Deviled Duck Eggs, 112
Deviled Quail Eggs & Caviar, 115
Luxe Truffle Deviled Eggs, 119

KIDS' PARTY

Let the kids pipe and top their own:
Garden Ranch 'n' Veggie Deviled Eggs, 50
Honey Mustard Deviled Eggs, 101

GAME DAY

Consider these for your menu's starting lineup:
Red-Hot Buffalo Deviled Eggs, 98
Steak & Deviled Eggs, 65
Honey Mustard Deviled Eggs, 101
Southwest Salsa Deviled Eggs, 48

CAESAR SALAD
page 130

BRUNCH
Serve an appetizer at brunch? Why not!
French Toast Deviled Eggs, 75
Bloody Mary Deviled Eggs, 79
Steak & Deviled Eggs, 65
Bacon Cheddar Deviled Eggs, 94
Brunchy Deviled "Eggs Benedict," 77

GIRLS NIGHT
Getting together with the girls?
Caesar Salad Deviled Eggs, 130
"California Roll" Deviled Eggs, 85
Fennel, Orange & Harissa Deviled Eggs, 111
Dirty Martini Deviled Eggs, 80

GUYS' NIGHT
Looking for man-food deviled eggs?
Steak & Deviled Eggs, 65
Bacon Cheddar Deviled Eggs, 94
Honey Mustard Deviled Eggs, 101
Old-School Onion Dip Deviled Eggs, 102
Red-Hot Buffalo Deviled Eggs, 98

BIRTHDAY
Celebrate the guest of honor with:
Retro Shrimp Cocktail Deviled Eggs, 82
Goat Cheese & Peppadew Deviled Eggs, 67
Tapenade Deviled Eggs, 56

BABY SHOWER
Bring a delicate touch to your menu:
Radishes & Butter Deviled Eggs, 133
Fennel, Orange & Harissa Deviled Eggs, 111
Crab Louis Deviled Eggs, 129

BRIDAL SHOWER

Celebrate in style with:
Smoked Salmon Deviled Eggs with Sour Cream & Chives, 47
Fennel, Orange & Harissa Deviled Eggs, 111
Crab Louis Deviled Eggs, 129
Radishes & Butter Deviled Eggs, 133

WEDDING

For an elegant, stylish nuptial fete:
Beet'ing Heart Deviled Eggs, 125
Lobster Deviled Eggs, 116
Emerald Asparagus & Sweet Onion Deviled Eggs, 122
Luxe Truffle Deviled Eggs, 119

SUMMER PICNIC

Make the most of the warm weather by dining outdoors:
Classic Picnic–Style Deviled Eggs, 36
All-American Potato Salad Deviled Eggs, 68
BLT Deviled Eggs, 53

PATIO BBQ

Fire up the grill and whip up a batch of:
Buttered Corn Deviled Eggs, 72
Glorious Greek Deviled Eggs, 59
Chipotle Deviled Eggs, 127

GAME OR MOVIE NIGHT

*Put a winning spin on the game
or whip up a blockbuster bite:*
Red-Hot Buffalo Deviled Eggs, 98
Pimiento Cheese Deviled Eggs, 104
Indian Curry Deviled Eggs, 107
Buttered Corn Deviled Eggs, 72

CLASSIC PICNIC–STYLE
page 36

THE HARD FACTS

ALL *about* EGGS

✤ I wish I had known the most important "hard fact" about hard-cooked eggs when I had my first big catering job in college—never use superfresh eggs, because they will not peel!

✤ But before we jump into cooking and peeling eggs, we've got to talk about choosing and purchasing them. If you've ever puzzled over the differences between brown eggs and white eggs, wonder no longer: there aren't any. Aside from the fact that brown eggs come from red and brown chickens, and white eggs come from white chickens, the eggs are virtually identical these days in size, taste, and nutritional value. This wasn't always the case; before large-scale production, brown eggs used to be slightly higher in nutrients simply because red and brown varieties of chickens tended to be larger, and therefore consumed more food than white chickens. Today, conventionally farmed chickens are fed the same diet regardless of variety.

✤ There are many types of eggs available today, and the choices can be dizzying. Grocery-store brands, farmers' markets, organic, free-range, cage-free . . . with the recent rise in popularity of backyard chicken keeping, you can even get eggs from your neighbor down the street. Where do you start? Most of these options have to do with personal choices in where your food comes from and the environment the chickens inhabit, but those factors can also make a difference in taste. Chickens that have been allowed to forage for their food and eat a predominantly wild diet will produce richer, more flavorful eggs. Whichever eggs you choose, be sure to look them over before purchase to ensure they are clean and free of cracks.

❖ There are a number of options when it comes to size; eggs are available from "peewee" to "jumbo" and a number of sizes in between. The recipes in this book were made with standard large eggs.

❖ For easy peeling, hard-cook eggs that have been refrigerated for at least seven to ten days. This allows time for the egg to take in some air, which helps separate the membrane from the shell. Store your eggs small end up or on their sides overnight before hard-cooking; this helps center the yolk.

❖ When it comes to boiling eggs, the most frequent problem is that people often overcook them. This leads to a dark green ring around the yolk and a funky, sulfurous taste. The following recipes for hard-cooking eggs, if followed carefully, will ensure flawlessly done eggs every time.

❖ We cooked one dozen eggs at a time, in a single layer, to prevent the eggs from cracking against each other. For the following methods, do not stack your eggs more than two layers deep. See the recipe Large-Batch Deviled Eggs Recipe Template, 139, to make larger quantities for special events or catering.

HOW TO

HARD-COOKED EGGS

20TH CENTURY–STYLE
page 43

CHICKEN
1 dozen large chicken eggs
Place the eggs in a large nonreactive saucepan and add cold water to 1 inch above the eggs. Bring to a boil over medium-high heat. Remove the pan from the heat and immediately cover. Let the eggs sit covered for 15 minutes, then run cold water over the eggs in the pan until they are cooled. When cool, carefully peel them under running water.

DUCK
1 dozen duck eggs
Place the eggs in a large nonreactive saucepan and add cold water to 1 inch above the eggs. Bring to a boil over medium-high heat. Remove the pan from the heat and immediately cover. Let the eggs sit covered for 18 minutes, then run cold water over the eggs in the pan until they are cooled. When cool, carefully peel them under running water.

QUAIL
1 dozen quail eggs
1 tablespoon white distilled vinegar
Place the eggs in a small nonreactive saucepan and add the vinegar and cold water to 1 inch above the eggs. Remove the pan from the heat and immediately cover. Let the eggs sit covered for 5 minutes, then run cold water over the eggs in the pan until they are cooled. When cool, carefully peel them under running water.

❧ Now that you've got perfectly hard-cooked eggs, let's get crackin'! When peeling hard-cooked eggs, roll each egg on the counter to get the peel going, then peel under a slow stream of cold water. Make sure to peel your eggs over a colander in the sink, to catch all the shells. I like to save the shells, dry them out, and then dig them into my garden, or add them to compost.

❧ And don't worry if you lose an egg in the cooking or peeling process . . . you can always just add the yolk to the filling and eat the broken white! In fact, some of the recipes in this book use all twelve yolks, but only yield enough filling for twenty egg-white halves. Feel free to make a healthy snack out of the rest!

❖ Hard-cooked eggs can be kept unpeeled and refrigerated for up to one week in an egg carton or covered container, to avoid picking up refrigerator odors. Once you are ready to proceed, peel the eggs and make your filling. We suggest filling the eggs the day you are serving them, as they tend to dry out when refrigerated overnight. However, precut egg whites and filling can be prepared and refrigerated, separately, a day ahead. Just be sure to set your egg white halves on a nonreactive container or platter and cover tightly. Fillings can be put in a piping bag with both the tip and top end secured with rubber bands. This is a useful way to transport a lot of eggs to a party and makes filling them a breeze when you arrive.

❖ Once your eggs are filled, they will need to be covered with plastic wrap if they are not being served right away. Store the eggs in a glass baking dish or deviled-egg dish, with toothpicks poked in a few eggs to "tent" the plastic wrap covering.

❖ Any toppings should be added just before serving so that they stay fresh and bright. Such things as popcorn or pretzels, especially, need to go on at the last minute to preserve the crunch. When making toppings that have tiny cut veggies, the more petite you can make your cuts, the prettier your finished eggs will look.

FILLINGS & PIPING
❖ The best part of deviled eggs is always the filling, and getting smooth yolks can be achieved in a number of ways. The easiest method is to mash your yolks thoroughly with a fork, ensuring an even texture—and giving you a good arm workout in the process! Other effective ways to mash your yolks include using an electric mixer with a whip attachment (ideal for bigger batches), a potato masher, or even a ricer.

❖ How much or how little you season your filling depends on your own taste, but here are some things to keep in mind. Different brands of mayonnaise will vary widely in saltiness, so be sure to taste the filling

before adding more salt. Other ingredients, such as pesto, tapenade, some kinds of seafood, and cured meats, will all add saltiness as well.

❧ Mustards are a key ingredient in deviled eggs, from coarse-textured whole-grain and stone-ground country varieties to kicky Dijons and sharp yellow mustards. Each type has a distinctive role to play; be sure to use the kind specified in the recipe.

❧ The type of salt you choose will also have an effect on the final flavor of your filling; table salt has nearly twice the potency of flakier varieties such as kosher and some sea salts. For a salty finish, you can simply garnish your eggs with a sprinkle of coarse sea salt or other fun specialty varieties.

❧ Once you are happy with the filling, it's time to fill those eggs! Spoon-filled deviled eggs will have a more laid-back, rustic look to them, whereas eggs that have been filled with a piping bag present an elegant, uniform impression.

❧ For piping, a number of different options are available. Standard cake decorating bags are ideal if you have them on hand. Disposable plastic piping bags are readily available in the baking section of most grocery stores and cake decorating shops and save on cleanup time. And if you're in a pinch for a piping bag, just use a plastic sandwich bag by simply cutting off the corner tip!

❧ The tip you pipe the filling with is largely an aesthetic choice, although some fillings are better suited to certain tip styles than others. Chunkier fillings would be best piped through a large plain round tip, while smoother fillings look lovely when applied with a large star tip.

❧ Fit the tip into the piping bag, and then fill the bag not more than two-thirds full to prevent any filling from oozing out the top. When filling the bag, fold down the top to maintain enough space to twist the end closed. This also helps keep things tidy.

❖ Once the bag is filled, and the top either twisted tightly closed or tied off with an elastic band or twist tie, hold the top of the bag with your dominant hand and guide with the other. Squeezing from the top of the bag will ensure consistent pressure, and give you more uniformly filled eggs.

TOPPINGS & GARNISHES

❖ Most of the recipes in this book have some sort of garnish, whether it's a sprinkle of herbs or a crispy topping. Garnishes should make sense and have something to do with the dish—or in this case, the egg. Elements of the filling can be used, such as in the Emerald Asparagus & Sweet Onion Deviled Eggs, 122, where a tender asparagus tip is the topper. Play with contrasting sensations, as in the spicy Chipotle Deviled Eggs, 127, which get diced fresh tomatoes tossed with fresh cilantro to balance out the heat.

❖ When thinking up garnishes, playing with texture is a surefire way to add contrast. Pair up a smooth and creamy filling with something super-crunchy; for example, the Honey Mustard Deviled Eggs, 101, have crushed pretzels sprinkled on top.

❖ If you're like me, and you love getting really creative with garnishes, try something whimsical. The French Toast Deviled Eggs, 75, are an excellent example; the miniature French toast pieces on top add a playful finish to the maple syrup and breakfast sausage–studded filling.

❖ Traditional deviled eggs that have no sweet notes can benefit from a savory item on top. Smoked oysters, cooked shrimp, or even twisted slices of artisan salami are delicious choices. Country Classic Deviled Eggs, 40, or 20th Century–Style Deviled Eggs, 43, are winning candidates for this kind of custom garnishing.

❖ As always, recipes are a guide; feel free to let your taste buds lead the way to putting a personal spin on these D'Lish Deviled Eggs.

GENERAL RECIPE NOTES

❖ When making a recipe for the first time, be sure to read it all the way through. Next, get all your ingredients together. I like to measure, slice, and dice everything ahead of time, basically making a "kit," then double-check the ingredients one last time before I start cooking.

❖ Cooking is an art, not a science; burners and ovens vary, as do ingredients from different parts of the country, and of the world, for that matter. High altitude definitely affects hard-cooking eggs. Use your best judgment when making the recipes in this book. Be sure to taste for seasoning, and if you fancy a bit more salt or spice, then add it to your liking.

INGREDIENTS
❖ Bell peppers are seeded and deribbed.
❖ Butter is salted.
❖ Chiles are seeded and deribbed, but if you like more heat, leave in the seeds and ribs.
❖ Crabmeat: Generally, there is no need to pick through purchased fresh Dungeness or King crabmeat for shell particles; if you are substituting lump or another crabmeat, be sure to do so.
❖ Cream is heavy whipping cream.
❖ Eggs are large.
❖ Garlic is always fresh—not the kind in a jar!
❖ Ginger is fresh and peeled.
❖ Green onion: The whole green onion is used.
❖ Herbs are fresh unless the recipe specifies dried. To substitute dried herbs for fresh, use only one-third to half as much; but substitute only if you're in a pinch, as this will greatly affect a recipe's flavor.
❖ Mayonnaise is regular, but can be replaced with low-fat or lite.
❖ Paprika is available in a range of pungency from sweet to hot, and smoked Spanish paprika (pimentón) is available sweet, bittersweet, or hot; if not specified in the recipe, use what you like.
❖ Parsley can be either Italian (flat-leaf) or curly; use what you like.
❖ Pepper, if not specified otherwise, is freshly ground black pepper.

❖ "Season to taste" means for you to taste the dish and then adjust the seasoning by adding more salt if you so desire, and pepper if the recipe indicates pepper.

❖ Sour cream is regular but can be replaced with low-fat.

❖ Soy sauce is regular-strength Japanese-style soy sauce, such as Kikkoman.

❖ "Store refrigerated" means to cover or wrap with plastic wrap before refrigerating, unless otherwise noted. (Be sure food has cooled before covering.)

❖ Yogurt is plain, unsweetened yogurt. Greek yogurt can also be used, and may be specified in the recipe.

AN IMPORTANT NOTE ON SALT

We used standard table salt in these recipes. Most chefs prefer kosher and/or sea salt and often use these rather than table salt. You'd be surprised at the difference in taste and texture from one salt to the next; use what you have on hand, but you might want to consider adding kosher or sea salt to your cupboard if it's not already there. If using kosher salt rather than table salt, up the amount a bit.

CUTS

❖ Mince: To cut into very small pieces, about ⅛ inch or smaller.

❖ Finely mince: ¹⁄₁₆ inch or smaller.

❖ Chop: To cut into ¼- to ½-inch irregular pieces that have a rustic look; pieces are not precisely cubed. Finely chop: ⅛- to ¼-inch pieces.

❖ Coarsely chop: ½-inch rough-cut pieces, except when referring to fresh herbs, such as flat-leaf parsley, and small foods, such as nuts or olives; in those cases, "coarsely chop" means rough-cutting into about ¼-inch pieces.

❖ Dice: To cut foods into small cubes; the very even cuts make for even cooking and an appealing look; the size is usually specified, for example, ¼ or ½ inch. Small dice is ¼ inch. Very tiny dice is ⅛ inch.

❖ Julienne: To cut into even, matchstick-sized strips, 1 to 3 inches long, and ¹⁄₁₆-inch square in cross-section, or the specified size.

✤ To make crème fraîche: If you cannot locate it, you can make your own. Combine 1 cup of sour cream and 2 cups of heavy cream in a large glass jar. Tighten the lid and shake to mix thoroughly. Set in a warm place for 8 to 24 hours, until thickened. Store refrigerated.

✤ To make lemon or other citrus zest: Zest is the outer peel of the fruit—with no white pith attached. You can remove the zest from the fruit with a fine zesting tool that makes long, very thin, pretty strands. Or you can peel off the zest with an ordinary potato peeler, being sure not to get any white pith, and then finely cut the zest in very, very thin, long strips, or mince it. You can also grate it off. For this method, I like to use a Microplane.

✤ To toast nuts: Spread them on a baking sheet and toast in a preheated 350°F oven for 6 to 8 minutes, or until golden.

✤ To toast whole spices and seeds: Spread the seeds in a dry skillet over medium heat and lightly toast them, stirring frequently, until fragrant. Pour them into a pie pan or other flat dish to stop the cooking. This technique is commonly used for sesame, cumin, and coriander seed.

✤ Crush seeds or whole spices in a mortar or, if you don't have one, you can put them in a small, not-too-flimsy plastic bag, close it, place it on a cutting board, and crush the seeds with a mallet or even a hammer.

✤ Raw eggs, raw fish, and raw shellfish are not recommended for pregnant women, children, the elderly, or anyone with immune deficiencies.

HOW TO

33

RADISHES & BUTTER
page 133

RECIPES

CLASSIC PICNIC-STYLE DEVILED EGGS

Makes 24

Everybody has their go-to deviled-egg recipe; this is my take on the quintessential family party tradition. I wanted to include an example that really highlights the familiar deviled-egg flavors, but you can try substituting celery salt for a bit of a twist.

1 dozen hard-cooked eggs (page 25)

FILLING
¼ cup mayonnaise
1 tablespoon prepared yellow mustard
¼ teaspoon salt
¼ teaspoon freshly ground black pepper
2 tablespoons sweet pickle relish
1 tablespoon minced white onion
1 tablespoon minced celery

TOPPING
Paprika
2 tablespoons chopped fresh parsley

Halve the eggs lengthwise and transfer the yolks to a mixing bowl. Set the egg white halves on a platter, cover, and refrigerate.

With a fork, mash the yolks to a smooth consistency. Add the mayonnaise, mustard, salt, and pepper, and mix until smooth. (You can also do this using an electric mixer with a whip attachment.) Stir in the relish, onion, and celery. Taste and season accordingly.

Spoon the mixture into a pastry bag fitted with a plain or large star tip, then pipe the mixture evenly into the egg white halves. Or fill the eggs with a spoon, dividing the filling evenly.

Top each egg half with a sprinkle of paprika and parsley.

GRANDMA'S OLD-FASHIONED DEVILED EGGS

Makes 24

In this earlier-style recipe, mustard powder, white vinegar, and sugar give a bright little pop of sweet-and-sour goodness. My grandmother Mimi often made these for Sunday suppers; we could hardly keep our hands off the eggs until it was time to eat.

1 dozen hard-cooked eggs (page 25)

FILLING
½ teaspoon sugar
½ teaspoon vinegar
½ teaspoon Colman's mustard powder
6 tablespoons mayonnaise
1 teaspoon prepared yellow mustard
¼ teaspoon salt
1 tablespoon minced white onion
1 tablespoon minced celery

TOPPING
24 tiny celery leaves

Halve the eggs lengthwise and transfer the yolks to a mixing bowl. Set the egg white halves on a platter, cover, and refrigerate.

In a small bowl, stir together the sugar, vinegar, and mustard powder, then mix in the mayonnaise and mustard.

With a fork, mash the yolks to a smooth consistency. Add the mayonnaise mixture and salt, and mix until smooth. (You can also do this using an electric mixer with a whip attachment.) Stir in the onion and celery. Taste and season accordingly.

Spoon the mixture into a pastry bag fitted with a plain or large star tip, then pipe the mixture evenly into the egg white halves. Or fill the eggs with a spoon, dividing the filling evenly.

Top each egg half with a celery leaf.

COUNTRY CLASSIC DEVILED EGGS

Makes 24

The tiny seeds in stone-ground mustard, often called country mustard, add textural interest to the filling. There's something about deviled eggs and sunny days that just go oh-so-well together. For me, this version invokes fond memories of warm summer picnics and festive neighborhood potlucks.

1 dozen hard-cooked eggs (page 25)

FILLING
6 tablespoons mayonnaise
1 tablespoon stone-ground mustard
¼ teaspoon salt
⅛ teaspoon freshly ground black pepper
2 tablespoons thinly sliced green onion
2 tablespoons minced celery

TOPPING
2 tablespoons thinly sliced green onion

Halve the eggs lengthwise and transfer the yolks to a mixing bowl. Set the egg white halves on a platter, cover, and refrigerate.

With a fork, mash the yolks to a smooth consistency. Add the mayonnaise, mustard, salt, and pepper, and mix until smooth. (You can also do this using an electric mixer with a whip attachment.) Stir in the green onion and celery. Taste and season accordingly.

Spoon the mixture into a pastry bag fitted with a plain or large star tip, then pipe the mixture evenly into the egg white halves. Or fill the eggs with a spoon, dividing the filling evenly.

Top each egg half with a sprinkle of green onion.

20TH CENTURY–STYLE DEVILED EGGS

Makes 24

This is my retro riff: Horseradish, that midcentury darling, adds a little kick to the mix; and minced baby dill pickles take the place of prepared relish for a nice crunch factor. These eggs would be excellent topped with crab, shrimp, smoked oysters, or clams.

1 dozen hard-cooked eggs (page 25)

FILLING
6 tablespoons mayonnaise
1 tablespoon prepared horseradish
¾ teaspoon Dijon mustard
½ teaspoon Worcestershire sauce
¼ teaspoon salt
¼ teaspoon freshly ground black pepper
2 tablespoons minced baby dill pickles
1 tablespoon finely chopped fresh parsley

TOPPING
24 thin-sliced rounds baby dill pickle
1 tablespoon jarred diced pimiento (or very tiny-diced red pepper)

Halve the eggs lengthwise and transfer the yolks to a mixing bowl. Set the egg white halves on a platter, cover, and refrigerate.

With a fork, mash the yolks to a smooth consistency. Add the mayonnaise, horseradish, mustard, Worcestershire, salt, and pepper, and mix until smooth. (You can also do this using an electric mixer with a whip attachment.) Stir in the minced dill pickles and parsley. Taste and season accordingly.

Spoon the mixture into a pastry bag fitted with a plain or large star tip, then pipe the mixture evenly into the egg white halves. Or fill the eggs with a spoon, dividing the filling evenly. Top each egg half with a slice of dill pickle and about ⅛ teaspoon of the diced pimiento.

❖ TIP ❖
Be sure to use prepared horseradish, rather than creamed horseradish.

EASY ROASTED GARLIC 'N' HERB DEVILED EGGS

Makes 24

These eggs make a fabulous first course for an evening of Italian cuisine. They could also shine alongside a tasty plate of prosciutto and olives or be a welcome companion to good conversation and a glass of wine. Whip these up in no time with the microwave method of roasting garlic in oil.

1 dozen hard-cooked eggs (page 25)

FILLING
2 tablespoons olive oil
¼ cup whole garlic cloves
¼ cup mayonnaise
1 tablespoon crème fraîche or sour cream
1 tablespoon country Dijon mustard
½ teaspoon minced fresh rosemary
1 teaspoon minced fresh thyme
1 tablespoon thinly sliced fresh chives
1 tablespoon minced shallots
¼ teaspoon salt
Freshly ground black pepper

TOPPING
2 tablespoons coarsely chopped fresh Italian parsley
24 tiny fresh thyme sprigs

Halve the eggs lengthwise and transfer the yolks to a mixing bowl, and reserve. Set the egg white halves on a platter, cover, and refrigerate.

In a small microwavable custard cup or dish, combine the olive oil and garlic. Cover the dish with plastic wrap and puncture it. Microwave for about 2 minutes, or until the garlic is tender. Let cool, and then drain the garlic, reserving the oil. Mash the garlic into a smooth paste.

With a fork, mash the reserved yolks to a smooth consistency. Add the mayonnaise, crème fraîche, garlic paste, reserved garlic oil, mustard, herbs, shallots, and salt, and mix until smooth. (You can also do this using an electric mixer with a whip attachment.) Add black pepper to taste.

Spoon the mixture into a pastry bag fitted with a plain or large star tip, then pipe the mixture evenly into the egg white halves. Or fill the eggs with a spoon, dividing the filling evenly.

Top each egg half with a sprinkle of parsley and a sprig of thyme.

SMOKED SALMON DEVILED EGGS WITH SOUR CREAM & CHIVES

Makes 24

You can use either hard- or cold-smoked salmon in these elegant but surprisingly easy stuffed eggs. If you are using cold-smoked salmon or lox, a tiny piece on top of each egg adds extra flair. Pair these up with a gorgeous fresh arugula and roasted beet salad. Now, that's a lunch!

1 dozen hard-cooked eggs (page 25)

FILLING

3 tablespoons mayonnaise
3 tablespoons regular or low-fat sour cream
½ teaspoon Dijon mustard
1 teaspoon minced fresh garlic
¼ teaspoon salt
2 tablespoons thinly sliced fresh chives
2 ounces (¼ cup) minced smoked salmon

TOPPING

3 tablespoons thinly sliced fresh chives
3 tablespoons finely minced red onion
1 tablespoon seasoned rice vinegar (optional)

Halve the eggs lengthwise and transfer the yolks to a mixing bowl. Set the egg white halves on a platter, cover, and refrigerate.

With a fork, mash the yolks to a smooth consistency. Add the mayonnaise, sour cream, mustard, garlic, and salt, and mix until smooth. (You can also do this using an electric mixer with a whip attachment.) Stir in the chives and salmon until evenly mixed in. Taste and season accordingly.

Spoon the mixture into a pastry bag fitted with a large plain tip, then pipe the mixture evenly into the egg white halves. Or fill the eggs with a spoon, dividing the filling evenly. To make the topping, in a small bowl, mix the chives, onion, and vinegar, if desired. Top each egg half with about ¾ teaspoon of the mixture.

SOUTHWEST SALSA DEVILED EGGS

Makes 24

Sure, you could put out plain old chips and salsa next time you have friends and family over . . . or, you could serve up these tasty Tex-Mex eggs. They've got lots of goodies and a ton of sassy style. Fire up the grill, crank up the tunes, and you've got a party on your hands.

1 dozen hard-cooked eggs (page 25)

FILLING
2 tablespoons mayonnaise
2 tablespoons sour cream
½ cup shredded sharp Cheddar cheese
¼ cup thick-and-chunky-style salsa
2 teaspoons hot sauce
½ teaspoon chili powder
¼ teaspoon salt

TOPPING
½ cup crushed tortilla chips
½ lime
2 tablespoons sour cream
24 thin slices fresh jalapeño
24 tiny fresh cilantro leaves

Halve the eggs lengthwise and transfer the yolks to a mixing bowl. Set the egg white halves on a platter, cover, and refrigerate.

With a fork, mash the yolks to a smooth consistency. Add the mayonnaise, sour cream, Cheddar cheese, salsa, hot sauce, chili powder, and salt, and mix until smooth. (You can also do this using an electric mixer with a whip attachment.) Taste and season accordingly.

Spoon the mixture into a pastry bag fitted with a large plain tip, then pipe the mixture evenly into the egg white halves. Or fill the eggs with a spoon, dividing the filling evenly.

Place the crushed chips in a small bowl and squeeze the lime over them. Toss to coat. Top each egg with ¼ teaspoon of the sour cream, a small pouf of chips, a slice of jalapeño, and a cilantro leaf.

GARDEN RANCH 'N' VEGGIE DEVILED EGGS

Makes 24

Whether it's after-school snack time or a backyard birthday party, these tasty little eggs are easy to make with the kids. Let them help garnish; little hands will love sprinkling on the colorful, crunchy veggie topping.

1 dozen hard-cooked eggs (page 25)

FILLING
½ cup premade ranch dressing
1 tablespoon chopped fresh parsley

TOPPING
1 tablespoon very tiny-diced red bell pepper
2 tablespoons very tiny-diced celery
2 tablespoons very tiny-diced carrot
2 tablespoons premade ranch dressing

Halve the eggs lengthwise and transfer the yolks to a mixing bowl. Set the egg white halves on a platter, cover, and refrigerate.

With a fork, mash the yolks to a smooth consistency. Add the ranch dressing and parsley, and mix until smooth. (You can also do this using an electric mixer with a whip attachment.) Taste and season accordingly.

Spoon the mixture into a pastry bag fitted with a plain or large star tip, then pipe the mixture evenly into the egg white halves. Or fill the eggs with a spoon, dividing the filling evenly.

To make the topping, in a small bowl, mix the bell pepper, celery, and carrot together. Top each egg half with ¼ teaspoon of the ranch dressing and a sprinkle of the veggie mixture.

BLT DEVILED EGGS

Makes 24

*The iconic sandwich turns devilish. Juicy tomatoes and crisp lettuce add a
fresh finish, but the real star of this show is bacon—even the drippings are
swirled into the filling so you don't miss out on any bacony goodness. If you
like a little extra heat, try using peppered bacon.*

1 dozen hard-cooked eggs (page 25)

FILLING
4 strips bacon, minced (about ½ cup, packed)
Mayonnaise, as needed to make ½ cup with bacon drippings
¼ teaspoon salt
⅛ teaspoon freshly ground black pepper

TOPPING
¼ cup fincly chopped lettuce
6 cherry tomatoes, sliced into 4 rounds each
Coarse salt and freshly ground black pepper

Halve the eggs lengthwise, transfer the yolks to a mixing bowl, and
reserve. Set the egg white halves on a platter, cover, and refrigerate.

In a medium skillct or sauté pan over medium to medium-high heat,
sauté the bacon until crispy, about 5 minutes; do not scorch. Drain
the drippings into a heatproof measuring cup, and reserve the bacon
separately. Let cool. To the cooled drippings, add mayonnaise as
needed to make ½ cup total.

With a fork, mash the reserved yolks to a smooth consistency. Add the
mayonnaise and drippings mixture, salt, and pepper, and mix until
smooth. (You can also do this using an electric mixer with a whip
attachment.) Stir in the reserved bacon. Taste and season accordingly.

Spoon the mixture into a pastry bag fitted with a large plain tip, then
pipe the mixture evenly into the egg white halves. Or fill the eggs with
a spoon, dividing the filling evenly. Top each egg half with a small
pouf of lettuce, 1 slice of tomato, and a sprinkle of salt and freshly
ground pepper.

THAI CURRY-SPICED DEVILED EGGS WITH SHRIMP

Makes 24

The rich, aromatic flavors of Thailand inspired these spicy eggs. The mint and cilantro bring a fresh pop to the garnish. To switch out the peanuts but still keep the crunchy goodness, you can use tiny-diced water chestnuts.

1 dozen hard-cooked eggs (page 25)

FILLING
½ cup mayonnaise
2 teaspoons Dijon mustard
2 teaspoons Thai yellow curry paste (see Tip)
1 teaspoon minced fresh garlic
1 teaspoon minced fresh ginger
¼ teaspoon Tabasco sauce
¼ cup finely chopped cooked salad shrimp

TOPPING
⅓ cup finely chopped cooked salad shrimp
1 tablespoon chopped fresh cilantro
1 tablespoon chopped fresh mint
2 tablespoons chopped unsalted roasted peanuts

Halve the eggs lengthwise and transfer the yolks to a mixing bowl. Set the egg white halves on a platter, cover, and refrigerate.

With a fork, mash the yolks to a smooth consistency. Add the mayonnaise, mustard, curry paste, garlic, ginger, and Tabasco sauce, and mix until smooth. (You can also do this using an electric mixer with a whip attachment.) Stir in the chopped shrimp. Taste and season accordingly.

Spoon the mixture into a pastry bag fitted with a large plain tip, then pipe the mixture evenly into the egg white halves. Or fill the eggs with a spoon, dividing the filling evenly.

To make the topping, in a small bowl, mix together the shrimp, cilantro, and mint. Top each egg half with a heaping ½ teaspoon of the mixture. Sprinkle with peanuts.

❖ TIP ❖
Yellow curry paste is available at well-stocked grocers and Asian markets. I like the Mae Ploy brand.

TAPENADE DEVILED EGGS

Makes 24

This recipe uses homemade tapenade, but if you're short on time, you can use a high-quality purchased product instead. For Halloween, rename this recipe "Ghoulish Rotten Eggs." Garnish with soaked basil seeds (see Tip) to look like tiny eyeballs. Either way, these are sure to be the belle of the Monster's Ball!

1 dozen hard-cooked eggs (page 25)

FILLING
¼ cup mayonnaise
½ teaspoon balsamic vinegar
½ cup Black Olive Tapenade (recipe follows)

TOPPING
¼ cup Black Olive Tapenade (recipe follows)
24 small fresh basil leaves

Halve the eggs lengthwise and transfer the yolks to a mixing bowl. Set the egg white halves on a platter, cover, and refrigerate.

With a fork, mash the yolks to a smooth consistency. Add the mayonnaise and balsamic vinegar and mix until smooth. (You can also do this using an electric mixer with a whip attachment.) Stir in the tapenade. Taste and season accordingly.

Spoon the mixture into a pastry bag fitted with a plain or large star tip, then pipe the mixture evenly into the egg white halves. Or fill the eggs with a spoon, dividing the filling evenly.

Top each egg half with about ½ teaspoon of the tapenade and a basil leaf.

❖ TIP ❖

To soak basil seeds, combine ½ teaspoon of seeds with 2 tablespoons of water. Let soak for 10 to 12 minutes, until "plumped." Basil seeds are available at Asian grocery stores or online. If using basil seeds from gardening packets, be sure to purchase organic seeds.

BLACK OLIVE TAPENADE
Makes ¾ cup, enough for 1 recipe

½ cup pitted kalamata olives
½ cup pitted black ripe olives
1 tablespoon extra-virgin olive oil
1 tablespoon minced fresh garlic

In a food processor, combine all the ingredients and process until finely chopped but still with some nice texture. Refrigerate until needed.

GLORIOUS GREEK DEVILED EGGS

Makes 24

Mediterranean flavors mingle in this Greek-inspired deviled egg. If you grow fresh oregano in your garden, be sure to switch it for the dry. If you're lucky enough to have your oregano blooming when you make these, garnish your eggs with the beautiful, tiny purple flowers.

1 dozen hard-cooked eggs (page 25)

FILLING
3 tablespoons mayonnaise
3 tablespoons plain Greek yogurt
1 tablespoon minced fresh garlic
1 teaspoon dried whole oregano, or 2 teaspoons fresh
¼ teaspoon red pepper flakes
¼ teaspoon salt
2 tablespoons minced pepperoncini

TOPPING
2 tablespoons very tiny-diced red bell pepper
2 tablespoons very tiny-diced kalamata olives
⅓ cup crumbled feta cheese
1 tablespoon minced fresh parsley

Halve the eggs lengthwise and transfer the yolks to a mixing bowl. Set the egg white halves on a platter, cover, and refrigerate.

With a fork, mash the yolks to a smooth consistency. Add the mayonnaise, yogurt, garlic, oregano, pepper flakes, and salt, and mix until smooth. (You can also do this using an electric mixer with a whip attachment.) Stir in the pepperoncini. Taste and season accordingly.

Spoon the mixture into a pastry bag fitted with a plain or large star tip, then pipe the mixture evenly into the egg white halves. Or fill the eggs with a spoon, dividing the filling evenly.

To make the topping, in a small bowl, mix together the bell pepper, olives, feta, and parsley. Top each egg half with about 1 teaspoon of the mixture.

FIRECRACKER BBQ PORK DEVILED EGGS

Makes 24

I love playing with Chinese BBQ pork's sweet and salty nature, especially pairing it up with an element of heat. Most of the time, when you purchase the pork, a small packet of Chinese hot mustard accompanies it; if so, use this in the filling.

1 dozen hard-cooked eggs (page 25)

FILLING
6 tablespoons mayonnaise
2 to 3 teaspoons Chinese hot mustard
¼ teaspoon salt
2 tablespoons thinly sliced green onion

TOPPING
1 tablespoon hoisin sauce
1 tablespoon ketchup
⅓ cup 1-inch julienned Chinese BBQ pork
1 tablespoon mixed, toasted, black and white sesame seeds

Halve the eggs lengthwise and transfer the yolks to a mixing bowl. Set the egg white halves on a platter, cover, and refrigerate.

With a fork, mash the yolks to a smooth consistency. Add the mayonnaise, mustard, and salt, and mix until smooth. (You can also do this using an electric mixer with a whip attachment.) Stir in the green onion. Taste and season accordingly.

Spoon the mixture into a pastry bag fitted with a plain or large star tip, then pipe the mixture evenly into the egg white halves. Or fill the eggs with a spoon, dividing the filling evenly.

To make the topping, in a tiny bowl, mix the hoisin sauce and ketchup. Top each egg half with a small pouf of BBQ pork, drizzle with ¼ teaspoon of the sauce mixture, and sprinkle with sesame seeds.

CORNED BEEF & SAUERKRAUT DEVILED EGGS

Makes 24

Corned beef and cabbage is, of course, an Irish tradition, but I couldn't resist putting my twist on it. I switched out boiled cabbage for the tartness of sauerkraut in these hearty and satisfying eggs, but threw in some horseradish as a little nod to the original.

1 dozen hard-cooked eggs (page 25)

FILLING
6 tablespoons mayonnaise
1 tablespoon prepared yellow mustard
1 tablespoon prepared horseradish (see Tip)
¼ teaspoon salt
½ cup finely chopped corned beef

TOPPING
¼ cup finely chopped cooked corned beef
¼ cup coarsely chopped sauerkraut, drained well

Halve the eggs lengthwise and transfer the yolks to a mixing bowl. Set the egg white halves on a platter, cover, and refrigerate.

With a fork, mash the yolks to a smooth consistency. Add the mayonnaise, mustard, horseradish, and salt, and mix until smooth. (You can also do this using an electric mixer with a whip attachment.) Stir in the corned beef. Taste and season accordingly.

Spoon the mixture into a pastry bag fitted with a large plain tip, then pipe the mixture evenly into the egg white halves. Or fill the eggs with a spoon, dividing the filling evenly.

To make the topping, in a small bowl, mix together the corned beef and sauerkraut. Top each egg half with 1 teaspoon of the mixture.

❧ TIP ❧
Be sure to use prepared horseradish instead of the creamed variety to get the full, spicy effect.

ARTI-PARM DEVILED EGGS

Makes 20

A favorite dip or sauce can be a great jumping-off point for creating a new recipe. Artichoke-Parmesan dip is a personal favorite of mine, so I turned it into a deviled egg! I highly recommend using artichokes from a grocery store salad bar whenever possible; or, if you can find them, frozen artichokes are a good option.

1 dozen hard-cooked eggs (page 25)

FILLING
6 tablespoons mayonnaise
½ teaspoon Dijon mustard
2 teaspoons minced fresh garlic
1 tablespoon grated Parmesan cheese
1 tablespoon minced red onion
1 tablespoon minced pickled jalapeños
¼ teaspoon salt
3 tablespoons well-drained, finely chopped artichoke hearts

TOPPING
⅓ cup thinly sliced artichoke hearts
2 tablespoons chopped fresh basil or parsley
3 tablespoons grated Parmesan cheese

Halve the eggs lengthwise and transfer the yolks to a mixing bowl. Set the egg white halves on a platter, cover, and refrigerate. With a fork, mash the yolks to a smooth consistency. Add the mayonnaise, mustard, garlic, cheese, red onion, jalapeños, and salt, and mix until smooth. (You can also do this using an electric mixer with a whip attachment.) Stir in the artichoke hearts.

Spoon the mixture into a pastry bag fitted with a large plain tip, then pipe the mixture evenly into the egg white halves. Or fill the eggs with a spoon, dividing the filling evenly.

To make the topping, in a small bowl, mix together the artichoke hearts, basil, and cheese. Top each egg half with about 1 teaspoon of the mixture.

63

STEAK & DEVILED EGGS

Makes 20

A.1. steak sauce adds big bold personality to the filling. Paired with thin slices of steak, this combo makes for a winning play on steak and eggs! Place these out for game day, or even breakfast or brunch, and watch them fly off the plate faster than you can say "medium-rare"!

1 dozen hard-cooked eggs (page 25)

FILLING
¼ cup mayonnaise
3 tablespoons A.1. sauce

TOPPING
1 (4-ounce) piece of steak
Salt and freshly ground black pepper
2 tablespoons A.1. sauce
2 tablespoons thinly sliced fresh chives

Halve the eggs lengthwise and transfer the yolks to a mixing bowl. Set 20 egg white halves on a platter, cover, and refrigerate. This recipe uses 12 egg yolks, but only yields enough filling for 20 halves; reserve the extra 4 whites for another use.

With a fork, mash the yolks to a smooth consistency. Add the mayonnaise and A.1. sauce and mix until smooth. (You can also do this using an electric mixer with a whip attachment.)

Spoon the mixture into a pastry bag fitted with a plain or large star tip, then pipe the mixture evenly into the egg white halves. Or fill the eggs with a spoon, dividing the filling evenly. Taste and season accordingly.

Cut the steak into three long strips, season with salt and pepper, and cook to medium-rare on a grill or in a nonstick sauté pan. Let rest. Cut each strip of steak on the bias into 8 pieces.

Top each egg half with a piece of steak, ¼ teaspoon of A.1. sauce, and a sprinkle of chives.

GOAT CHEESE & PEPPADEW DEVILED EGGS

Makes 24

This easy-to-make app takes its cue from stuffed pickled peppers. Creamy cheese, tangy-sweet peppers, and a hit of heat tango in this sexy deviled-egg combo. Topped with a Marcona almond for a touch of salty contrast, these bites are utterly cravable.

1 dozen hard-cooked eggs (page 25)

FILLING
3 to 4 ounces fresh goat cheese (chèvre) (about ½ cup)
¼ cup mayonnaise
1½ teaspoons Tabasco sauce
8 to 10 Peppadew peppers, drained well and finely chopped
   (about ¼ cup)

TOPPING
24 Marcona almonds
2 tablespoons minced fresh parsley

Halve the eggs lengthwise and transfer the yolks to a mixing bowl. Set the egg white halves on a platter, cover, and refrigerate.

With a fork, mash the yolks to a smooth consistency. Add the goat cheese, mayonnaise, and Tabasco sauce, and mix until smooth. (You can also do this using an electric mixer with a whip attachment.) Stir in the peppers. Taste and season accordingly.

Spoon the mixture into a pastry bag fitted with a plain or large star tip, then pipe the mixture evenly into the egg white halves. Or fill the eggs with a spoon, dividing the filling evenly.

Top each egg half with a Marcona almond and a sprinkle of parsley.

ALL-AMERICAN POTATO SALAD DEVILED EGGS

Makes 24

I often create a recipe out of some fond memory, and these eggs are the perfect example. I remember sitting in the backyard on a big old picnic blanket with a bowl of Grandmother's potato salad and a heaping plate of piping-hot fried chicken. What a yummy inspiration!

1 dozen hard-cooked eggs (page 25)

FILLING
6 tablespoons mayonnaise
2 tablespoons yellow mustard
1 teaspoon Worcestershire sauce
¼ teaspoon salt
¼ teaspoon freshly ground black pepper
1½ teaspoons sugar
1 tablespoon minced dill pickles
2 tablespoons minced red onion
2 tablespoons minced celery

TOPPING
1 tablespoon vinegar
1 tablespoon sugar
⅓ cup cooked small-diced potato
3 tablespoons finely chopped dill pickle
3 tablespoons chopped fresh parsley

Halve the eggs lengthwise and transfer the yolks to a mixing bowl. Set the egg white halves on a platter, cover, and refrigerate.

With a fork, mash the yolks to a smooth consistency. Add the mayonnaise, mustard, Worcestershire sauce, salt, pepper, and sugar, and mix until smooth. (You can also do this using an electric mixer with a whip attachment.) Stir in the pickles, onion, and celery. Taste and season accordingly.

Spoon the mixture into a pastry bag fitted with a plain or large star tip, then pipe the mixture evenly into the egg white halves. Or fill the eggs with a spoon, dividing the filling evenly.

To make the topping, in a small bowl, mix together the vinegar and sugar. Add the potato, pickle, and parsley, and toss until well coated. Top each egg half with about 1 heaping teaspoon of the mixture.

GREEN GODDESS DEVILED EGGS

Makes 24

Tarragon's anise notes and bright green personality bring an herbaceous attitude to these garden-fresh deviled eggs. For a truly classic Green Goddess flavor, replace the salt with 1 to 2 teaspoons of anchovy paste.

1 dozen hard-cooked eggs (page 25)

FILLING
½ ripe avocado
3 tablespoons mayonnaise
2 tablespoons sour cream
1 teaspoon minced fresh garlic
1 tablespoon chopped fresh tarragon
½ teaspoon salt

TOPPING
24 fresh tarragon leaves
Fresh-cracked black pepper

Halve the eggs lengthwise and transfer the yolks to a small bowl. Set the egg white halves on a platter, cover, and refrigerate.

In a mixing bowl, mash the avocado well with a fork, then add the yolks and mash to a smooth consistency. Add the mayonnaise, sour cream, garlic, tarragon, and salt, and mix until smooth. (You can also do this using an electric mixer with a whip attachment.) Taste and season accordingly.

Spoon the mixture into a pastry bag fitted with a plain or large star tip, then pipe the mixture evenly into the egg white halves. Or fill the eggs with a spoon, dividing the filling evenly.

Top each egg half with a tarragon leaf and a grind of fresh-cracked black pepper.

BUTTERED CORN DEVILED EGGS

Makes 20

If you love corn, these eggs are for you. From an outdoor grilling party to movie night, your appetizer spread just got more interesting. These eggs get "corny" with a bit of butter whipped into the filling along with grilled corn. Salty popcorn makes for a whimsical topping.

1 dozen hard-cooked eggs (page 25)

FILLING
4 tablespoons salted butter, softened
2 tablespoons mayonnaise
2 tablespoons sour cream
¼ teaspoon salt
½ cup Grilled Corn (recipe follows)

TOPPING
¼ cup Grilled Corn (recipe follows)
48 pieces salted popcorn (about 1½ cups)
2 tablespoons thinly sliced fresh chives

Halve the eggs lengthwise and transfer the yolks to a mixing bowl. Set the egg white halves on a platter, cover, and refrigerate.

In a mixing bowl with a whip attachment, whip together the yolks and butter until smooth. Add the mayonnaise, sour cream, and salt, and mix until smooth. Stir in the corn.

Spoon the mixture into a pastry bag fitted with a large plain tip, then pipe the mixture evenly into the egg white halves. Or fill the eggs with a spoon, dividing the filling evenly.

Top each egg half with about ½ teaspoon of grilled corn kernels, 2 pieces of popcorn and a sprinkle of chives.

GRILLED CORN
Makes about ¾ cup kernels, enough for 1 recipe

1 ear fresh corn, husked
2 teaspoons vegetable oil
1 teaspoon salt
Freshly ground black pepper
2 tablespoons thinly sliced fresh chives

Preheat a grill to medium-high. Rub the ear of corn with the oil.
Grill the corn for 4 to 5 minutes, or until lightly grill-marked, turning
frequently. Let cool. Trim the kernels from the cob, place in a small
bowl, and season lightly with salt and pepper. Stir in the chives.

❖ TIP ❖
*To cha-cha up this recipe, garnish each egg half with a small dot of hot
sauce, a squeeze of lime, a sprinkle of queso fresco, and a cilantro leaf.*

FRENCH TOAST DEVILED EGGS

Makes 24

These sweet-and-savory eggs brighten up any morning menu. Serve them paired with a mimosa for a breakfasty sip and app. Tiny pieces of "French toast" make for a charming and unique garnish.

1 dozen hard-cooked eggs (page 25)

FILLING
2 tablespoons mayonnaise
¼ cup sour cream
1 tablespoon real maple syrup
¼ teaspoon salt
¼ cup cooked, crumbled, breakfast sausage (about 2 ounces uncooked)

TOPPING
24 each Petit French Toast pieces (recipe follows)
1 tablespoon real maple syrup
24 very tiny half-slices of strawberry (optional)

Halve the eggs lengthwise and transfer the yolks to a mixing bowl. Set the egg white halves on a platter, cover, and refrigerate.

With a fork, mash the yolks to a smooth consistency. Add the mayonnaise, sour cream, maple syrup, and salt, and mix until smooth. (You can also do this using an electric mixer with a whip attachment.) Stir in the breakfast sausage. Taste and season accordingly.

Spoon the mixture into a pastry bag fitted with a large plain tip, then pipe the mixture evenly into the egg white halves. Or fill the eggs with a spoon, dividing the filling evenly.

Top each egg half with 1 piece of French toast and ⅛ teaspoon of maple syrup. Add a small piece of strawberry, if desired. »

PETIT FRENCH TOAST

Makes 24 pieces, enough for 1 recipe

1½ slices white bread
1 egg
1 tablespoon milk
2 teaspoons sugar
¼ teaspoon ground nutmeg
¼ teaspoon ground cinnamon

Cut the crust off the bread. Cut the whole slice into sixteen equal-sized squares, and the half-slice into eight. You should have two dozen tiny squares.

In a small bowl, whisk together the egg, milk, sugar, and spices.

Pour the egg mixture into a shallow pan or pie dish. Lay the bread squares on the egg mixture, then flip them over to coat well and absorb the egg mixture.

Meanwhile, heat a 10-inch nonstick sauté pan over medium heat. Spray with pan spray. Lay in the French toast pieces and cook for about 1 minute until light golden. Flip, and cook for about 1 more minute. Transfer to a plate or rack until ready to use. If making ahead, refrigerate, then bring to room temperature before garnishing the eggs.

BRUNCHY DEVILED "EGGS BENEDICT"

Makes 24

This book would not have been complete without a cheeky take on everyone's favorite brunch dish, Eggs Benedict. Of course, we had to scale it down, so we topped the eggs off with tiny toasted English muffin croutons and a drizzle of decadent hollandaise.

½ English muffin
1½ teaspoons salted butter
1 dozen hard-cooked eggs (page 25)

FILLING
½ cup prepared hollandaise sauce
1 teaspoon fresh lemon juice
¼ teaspoon salt
½ cup minced Canadian bacon (about 2½ ounces)

TOPPING
2 slices Canadian bacon
¼ cup prepared hollandaise sauce
Paprika

To make the croutons, toast the English muffin slice until very crispy in a toaster and then spread lightly with butter. Trim off the sides and then cut the muffin to make two dozen tiny square croutons. Set aside.

Halve the eggs lengthwise and transfer the yolks to a mixing bowl. Set the egg white halves on a platter, cover, and refrigerate.

With a fork, mash the yolks to a smooth consistency. Add the hollandaise sauce, lemon juice, and salt, and mix until smooth. (You can also do this using an electric mixer with a whip attachment.) Stir in the Canadian bacon. Taste and season accordingly.

Spoon the mixture into a pastry bag fitted with a large plain tip, then pipe the mixture evenly into the egg white halves. Or fill the eggs with a spoon, dividing the filling evenly.

Cut each slice of Canadian bacon into 12 wedges. Top each egg half with a piece of bacon, ½ teaspoon of hollandaise sauce, and an English muffin crouton. Sprinkle lightly with paprika.

❖ TIP ❖

*For an extra kick of
spicy flavor, use a
Microplane to shave
fresh horseradish
atop the eggs.*

BLOODY MARY DEVILED EGGS

Makes 24

These eggs transport the essence of the timeless cocktail into a delightful little appetizer. Whether it's a midmorning wake-up call or gracing the table at a cocktail-hour fete, you can definitely have more than one of these not-so-libatious treats. Be sure to use prepared rather than the milder creamed horseradish for the most impact.

1 dozen hard-cooked eggs (page 25)

FILLING
½ cup mayonnaise
1 tablespoon prepared horseradish
1 teaspoon Worcestershire sauce
½ teaspoon Tabasco sauce
¼ teaspoon celery seeds
¼ teaspoon salt

TOPPING
½ cup very tiny-diced tomatoes
2 tablespoons minced celery
4 teaspoons minced, pimiento-stuffed green olives
1 tablespoon fresh lemon juice
2 teaspoons vodka

Halve the eggs lengthwise and transfer the yolks to a mixing bowl. Set the egg white halves on a platter, cover, and refrigerate.

With a fork, mash the yolks to a smooth consistency. Add the mayonnaise, horseradish, Worcestershire sauce, Tabasco sauce, celery seeds, and salt, and mix until smooth. (You can also do this using an electric mixer with a whip attachment.) Taste and season accordingly.

Spoon the mixture into a pastry bag fitted with a plain or large star tip, then pipe the mixture evenly into the egg white halves. Or fill the eggs with a spoon, dividing the filling evenly. To make the topping, in a small bowl, mix together the tomatoes, celery, olives, lemon juice, and vodka. Top each egg half with about 1 teaspoon of the mixture.

DIRTY MARTINI DEVILED EGGS

Makes 20

I'm a fan of a good dirty martini, and these eggs certainly live up to their name. There are a ton of different gins out there you can use, but pick a juniper-forward gin to really bring home the "martini" experience.

1 dozen hard-cooked eggs (page 25)

FILLING
6 tablespoons mayonnaise
1 teaspoon Dijon mustard
1 tablespoon brine from pimiento-stuffed green olives
½ teaspoon Worcestershire sauce
¼ teaspoon salt
2 teaspoons finely minced shallots

TOPPING
1 tablespoon gin
¼ cup minced pimiento-stuffed green olives
1 teaspoon finely minced lemon zest
2 tablespoons minced cocktail onions
1 tablespoon chopped fresh parsley

Halve the eggs lengthwise and transfer the yolks to a mixing bowl. Set 20 egg white halves on a platter, cover, and refrigerate. This recipe uses 12 egg yolks, but only yields enough filling for 20 halves; reserve the extra 4 whites for another use.

With a fork, mash the yolks to a smooth consistency. Add the mayonnaise, mustard, olive brine, Worcestershire sauce, and salt, and mix until smooth. (You can also do this using an electric mixer with a whip attachment.) Stir in the shallots. Taste and season accordingly.

Spoon the mixture into a pastry bag fitted with a plain or large star tip, then pipe the mixture evenly into the egg white halves. Or fill the eggs with a spoon, dividing the filling evenly. To make the topping, in a small bowl, mix together the gin, olives, lemon zest, onions, and parsley. Top each egg half with about 1 teaspoon of the mixture.

❖ TIP ❖

*For a "dirtier"
flavor, before filling,
place the halved egg
whites cut side down
in a shallow dish
with 2 tablespoons of
gin mixed with ¼ cup
of olive brine. Let
soak for 1 to 2
hours, refrigerated.*

RETRO SHRIMP COCKTAIL DEVILED EGGS

Makes 24

What could possibly be done to improve shrimp cocktail, that beloved appetizer? Make it into a deviled egg, of course!

1 dozen hard-cooked eggs (page 25)

FILLING
¼ cup cream cheese, softened
2 tablespoons mayonnaise
½ cup finely chopped cooked salad shrimp
½ teaspoon salt
2 tablespoons minced celery

TOPPING
¼ cup Cocktail Sauce (recipe follows)
¼ cup finely chopped cooked salad shrimp
24 tiny celery leaves

Halve the eggs lengthwise and transfer the yolks to a mixing bowl. Set the egg white halves on a platter, cover, and refrigerate.

With a fork, mash the yolks to a smooth consistency. Add the cream cheese and mix well. Add the mayonnaise, shrimp, and salt, and mix until smooth. (You can also do this using an electric mixer with a whip attachment.) For a smoother consistency, blend all the ingredients in a food processor or blender until well combined. Stir in the celery. Taste and season accordingly.

Spoon the mixture into a pastry bag fitted with a large plain tip, then pipe the mixture evenly into the egg white halves. Or fill the eggs with a spoon, dividing the filling evenly.

Top each egg half with ½ teaspoon of cocktail sauce, ½ teaspoon of shrimp, and a celery leaf.

COCKTAIL SAUCE
Makes 1 heaping cup

1 cup tomato chili sauce
1 tablespoon prepared horseradish
1 tablespoon fresh lemon juice
1 teaspoon Worcestershire sauce
¼ teaspoon freshly ground black pepper

In a small bowl, stir together all the ingredients. Store refrigerated for up to 2 weeks.

❖ TIP ❖
This cool take on the cocktail-party staple features a quick and easy homemade cocktail sauce, but if you're in a hurry, you can always substitute store-bought.

❧ TIP ❧
To make tiny cucumber fans, quarter a
4-inch piece of English cucumber lengthwise.
Then cut each quarter into 18 thin slices—
the goal is to get 3 tiny slices per egg.

"CALIFORNIA ROLL" DEVILED EGGS

Makes 24

Part of the allure of sushi is the beautiful presentation, and these California roll–inspired eggs are dressed to impress. The lush wasabi and avocado filling whips up in no time, so you can spend a little longer making these eggs look like the work of art they are!

1 dozen hard-cooked eggs (page 25)

FILLING
½ ripe avocado
3 tablespoons mayonnaise
1 tablespoon purchased wasabi paste (or 1 tablespoon wasabi powder mixed with 1 tablespoon water)
¼ teaspoon salt

TOPPING
2 ounces crabmeat (⅓ to ½ cup)
24 small cucumber fans (see Tip)
Nori komi furikake (sesame seed–seaweed sprinkle)
2 tablespoons tobiko (flying fish roe)

Halve the eggs lengthwise and transfer the yolks to a small bowl. Set the egg white halves on a platter, cover, and refrigerate.

In a mixing bowl, mash the avocado well with a fork, then add the yolks and mash to a smooth consistency. Add the mayonnaise, wasabi paste, and salt, and mix until smooth. (You can also do this using an electric mixer with a whip attachment.) Taste and season accordingly.

Spoon the mixture into a pastry bag fitted with a plain or large star tip, then pipe the mixture evenly into the egg white halves. Or fill the eggs with a spoon, dividing the filling evenly.

Top each egg half with a little crabmeat, a cucumber fan, a sprinkle of furikake, and about ¼ teaspoon of tobiko.

DEVILISH GREEN EGGS & HAM

Makes 24

Kids and grown-ups alike will be charmed by the Seussian whimsy of these delicious deviled eggs; Sam-I-Am won't have to ask you twice whether you'd like these! If you have a favorite pesto recipe, by all means, use it in the filling.

1 dozen hard-cooked eggs (page 25)

FILLING

3 tablespoons mayonnaise
¾ teaspoon Dijon mustard
1 teaspoon minced fresh garlic
6 tablespoons purchased basil pesto
2 tablespoons very thinly sliced green onion
Salt

TOPPING

4 ounces very thinly sliced prosciutto, cut into short, thin strips
  (about ½ cup)
2 tablespoons finely chopped fresh basil
1 teaspoon extra-virgin olive oil

Halve the eggs lengthwise and transfer the yolks to a mixing bowl. Set the egg white halves on a platter, cover, and refrigerate.

With a fork, mash the yolks to a smooth consistency. Add the mayonnaise, mustard, garlic, and pesto, and mix until smooth. (You can also do this using an electric mixer with a whip attachment.) Stir in the green onion. Taste the egg mixture and add a little salt if needed; pestos differ in salt content.

Spoon the mixture into a pastry bag fitted with a plain or large star tip, then pipe the mixture evenly into the egg white halves. Or fill the eggs with a spoon, dividing the filling evenly.

To make the topping, in a small bowl, mix together the prosciutto and basil. Drizzle with the oil and toss to coat. Top each egg half with about 1 heaping teaspoon of the mixture.

GINGER CHILI DEVILED EGGS

Makes 24

Playing with warming and cooling elements is a great way to bring delicious contrast to a recipe. In these zingy deviled eggs, fragrant ginger dances with spicy Asian chili paste to heat up your mouth, and the English cucumber and aromatic cilantro topping cools it off.

1 dozen hard-cooked eggs (page 25)

FILLING
½ cup mayonnaise
2 teaspoons Dijon mustard
2 teaspoons sambal oelek (Asian hot chili paste)
1 teaspoon minced fresh garlic
2 teaspoons minced, peeled fresh ginger
¼ teaspoon salt

TOPPING
⅓ cup very thinly sliced, seeded, unpeeled English cucumber
2 tablespoons very thinly sliced red bell pepper
2 tablespoons chopped fresh cilantro
1½ teaspoons fresh lime juice

Halve the eggs lengthwise and transfer the yolks to a mixing bowl. Set the egg white halves on a platter, cover, and refrigerate.

With a fork, mash the yolks to a smooth consistency. Add the mayonnaise, mustard, sambal oelek, garlic, ginger, and salt, and mix until smooth. (You can also do this using an electric mixer with a whip attachment.) Taste and season accordingly.

Spoon the mixture into a pastry bag fitted with a plain or large star tip, then pipe the mixture evenly into the egg white halves.

To make the topping, in a small bowl, mix the cucumber, bell pepper, cilantro, and lime juice. Top each egg half with about 1 teaspoon of the mixture.

WASABI DEVILED EGGS

Makes 24

Wasabi, also known as Japanese horseradish, is a superbold flavor on its own. So in this recipe, I chose to complement it with a fresh, delicate cucumber topping. Pop a wasabi pea on each of these little green devils for a snappy finish.

1 dozen hard-cooked eggs (page 25)

FILLING
6 tablespoons mayonnaise
1 tablespoon purchased wasabi paste (or 1 tablespoon
   wasabi powder mixed with 1 tablespoon water)
2 tablespoons thinly sliced green onion
2 tablespoons very tiny-diced English cucumber

TOPPING
24 wasabi peas

Halve the eggs lengthwise and transfer the yolks to a mixing bowl. Set the egg white halves on a platter, cover, and refrigerate.

With a fork, mash the yolks to a smooth consistency. Add the mayonnaise and wasabi paste, and mix until smooth. (You can also do this using an electric mixer with a whip attachment.) Stir in the green onion and cucumber. Taste and season accordingly.

Spoon the mixture into a pastry bag fitted with a plain or large star tip, then pipe the mixture evenly into the egg white halves. Or fill the eggs with a spoon, dividing the filling evenly.

Top each egg half with a wasabi pea, whole or cracked.

BOURSIN & GARLIC DEVILED EGGS WITH HERB SALAD

Makes 24

Rich, creamy, and herby Boursin cheese provides instant character to these quick and easy eggs. Add a touch more garlic for extra punch. The hardest part will be acting as if they took all day!

1 dozen hard-cooked eggs (page 25)

FILLING
1 (5.5-ounce) package Boursin garlic-and-herb cheese
3 tablespoons mayonnaise
½ teaspoon minced fresh garlic
¼ teaspoon salt

TOPPING
⅓ cup herb salad (a mixture of torn fresh herbs, such as tarragon, chives, mint, Italian parsley, and basil)

Halve the eggs lengthwise and transfer the yolks to a mixing bowl. Set the egg white halves on a platter, cover, and refrigerate.

With a fork, mash the yolks to a smooth consistency. Add the cheese, mayonnaise, garlic, and salt, and mix until smooth. (You can also do this using an electric mixer with a whip attachment.) Taste and season accordingly.

Spoon the mixture into a pastry bag fitted with a plain or large star tip, then pipe the mixture evenly into the egg white halves. Or fill the eggs with a spoon, dividing the filling evenly.

Top each egg half with a pouf of herb salad.

BACON CHEDDAR DEVILED EGGS

Makes 24

Eggs, bacon, cheese . . . they go hand in hand. I really like this with sharp Cheddar, but use a milder version if you prefer. Serve these all-American eggs on their own as an app, or dish them up as a cool salad garnish. And as breakfasts on the fly go, these can't be beat.

1 dozen hard-cooked eggs (page 25)

FILLING
3 tablespoons mayonnaise
3 tablespoons sour cream
½ teaspoon Dijon mustard (optional)
1 teaspoon minced fresh garlic
¼ teaspoon salt
⅛ teaspoon freshly ground black pepper
⅓ cup finely grated sharp Cheddar cheese

TOPPING
¼ cup finely chopped crisp-cooked bacon
2 tablespoons very thinly sliced green onion
Freshly ground black pepper

Halve the eggs lengthwise and transfer the yolks to a mixing bowl. Set the egg white halves on a platter, cover, and refrigerate.

With a fork, mash the yolks to a smooth consistency. Add the mayonnaise, sour cream, mustard, if desired, garlic, salt, and pepper, and mix until smooth. (You can also do this using an electric mixer with a whip attachment.) Stir in the Cheddar until evenly mixed in. Taste and season accordingly.

Spoon the mixture into a pastry bag fitted with a large plain tip, then pipe the mixture evenly into the egg white halves. Or fill the eggs with a spoon, dividing the filling evenly.

To make the topping, in a small bowl, mix the bacon and green onion. Top each egg half with about ¾ teaspoon of the mixture, then sprinkle with black pepper.

CLAM'TASTIC DEVILED EGGS

Makes 24

Chopped clams are the star of these savory seaside bites. Substitute fresh steamed clams if you're at the beach or have access to them. For the ultimate garnish, top with tiny smoked clams. To kick up the clam factor, add 2 teaspoons of the clam nectar to the filling.

1 (6.5-ounce) can chopped clams
1 dozen hard-cooked eggs (page 25)

FILLING
3 tablespoons cream cheese
¼ cup mayonnaise
1 teaspoon Dijon mustard
¼ teaspoon salt
¼ teaspoon freshly ground black pepper
2 tablespoons thinly sliced green onion
2 tablespoons minced celery

TOPPING
Smoked paprika
1 tablespoon chopped fresh parsley

Drain the clams, mince, and set aside.

Halve the eggs lengthwise and transfer the yolks to a mixing bowl. Set the egg white halves on a platter, cover, and refrigerate.

In an electric mixer fitted with a whip attachment, mix the egg yolks on medium speed for 30 seconds. Add the cream cheese and combine until smooth. Then add the mayonnaise, mustard, salt, and pepper, and mix until smooth. Stir in the drained clams, green onion, and celery, and mix until well incorporated. Taste and season accordingly.

Spoon the mixture into a pastry bag fitted with a plain large tip, then pipe the mixture evenly into the egg white halves. Or fill the eggs with a spoon, dividing the filling evenly. Top each egg half with a sprinkle of paprika and parsley.

RED-HOT BUFFALO DEVILED EGGS

Makes 24

Look out! These game-time snacks are ready to play. Serve them up on Super Bowl Sunday for a winning alternative to wings and dip . . . chances are, they're a little tidier! To really pump up the blue cheese flavor, add a few crumbles on top of each egg.

1 dozen hard-cooked eggs (page 25)

FILLING
3 tablespoons mayonnaise
3 tablespoons sour cream
1 tablespoon Frank's RedHot Buffalo Wings sauce
2 tablespoons crumbled blue cheese
1 tablespoon chopped fresh parsley
¼ teaspoon celery salt (or substitute table salt)

TOPPING
2 tablespoons Frank's RedHot Buffalo Wings sauce
⅓ cup very tiny-diced celery
24 tiny celery leaves

Halve the eggs lengthwise and transfer the yolks to a mixing bowl. Set the egg white halves on a platter, cover, and refrigerate.

With a fork, mash the yolks to a smooth consistency. Add the mayonnaise, sour cream, Frank's sauce, blue cheese, parsley, and celery salt, and mix until smooth. (You can also do this using an electric mixer with a whip attachment.) Taste and season accordingly.

Spoon the mixture into a pastry bag fitted with a plain or large star tip, then pipe the mixture evenly into the egg white halves. Or fill the eggs with a spoon, dividing the filling evenly.

To make the topping, in a small bowl, mix Frank's sauce with the celery until well coated. Top each egg half with about 1 teaspoon of the mixture and a celery leaf.

HONEY MUSTARD DEVILED EGGS

Makes 20

Honey and mustard are like best friends in the snack world, and they definitely make life sweet (and salty) in these cravable deviled eggs. Texture is an excellent way to make your eggs memorable, so crush up some pretzels for the topping and you've got a bona fide treat on your hands.

1 dozen hard-cooked eggs (page 25)

FILLING
6 tablespoons mayonnaise
1 tablespoon prepared yellow mustard
1 tablespoon country Dijon mustard
2 tablespoons honey
¼ teaspoon salt

TOPPING
⅓ cup broken/crushed pretzel pieces

Halve the eggs lengthwise and transfer the yolks to a mixing bowl. Set 20 egg white halves on a platter, cover, and refrigerate. This recipe uses 12 egg yolks, but only yields enough filling for 20 halves; reserve the extra 4 whites for another use.

With a fork, mash the yolks to a smooth consistency. Add the mayonnaise, both mustards, honey, and salt, and mix until smooth. (You can also do this using an electric mixer with a whip attachment.) Taste and season accordingly.

Spoon the mixture into a pastry bag fitted with a plain or large star tip, then pipe the mixture evenly into the egg white halves. Or fill the eggs with a spoon, dividing the filling evenly.

Top each egg half with a sprinkle of pretzel pieces.

OLD-SCHOOL ONION DIP DEVILED EGGS

Makes 24

Okay, admit it . . . everyone loves retro onion dip! This throwback combines four (yes, four!) different forms of onion. It's always fun to showcase an ingredient by using it several different ways in the same dish. Just say, "Yum!" You know you want to.

1 dozen hard-cooked eggs (page 25)

FILLING
2 tablespoons mayonnaise
6 tablespoons sour cream
2 tablespoons Lipton onion soup mix
3 tablespoons minced white onion

TOPPING
⅓ cup French's French-fried onion pieces
2 tablespoons thinly sliced green onion

Halve the eggs lengthwise, transfer the yolks to a mixing bowl, and reserve. Set the egg white halves on a platter, cover, and refrigerate.

In a small bowl, combine the mayonnaise, sour cream, and soup mix, and mix until smooth. Let sit for 2 to 3 minutes. Meanwhile, with a fork, mash the yolks to a smooth consistency. Add the mayonnaise mixture to the yolks, and mash until smooth. (You can also do this using an electric mixer with a whip attachment.) Stir in the onion. Taste and season accordingly.

Spoon the mixture into a pastry bag fitted with a plain or large star tip, then pipe the mixture evenly into the egg white halves. Or fill the eggs with a spoon, dividing the filling evenly.

Top each egg half with sprinkles of fried onion and thinly sliced green onion.

PIMIENTO CHEESE DEVILED EGGS

Makes 24

Oh-so-Southern pimiento cheese is having a foodie revival, showing up everywhere from gourmet burgers to topping grilled shrimp. Serve these up on a Southern table spread with fried green tomatoes, Creole shrimp, and tall glasses of sweet tea.

1 dozen hard-cooked eggs (page 25)

FILLING
6 tablespoons shredded sharp Cheddar cheese
2 tablespoons cream cheese, softened
2 teaspoons minced fresh garlic
1 tablespoon minced pickled jalapeño
2 teaspoons Worcestershire sauce
2 teaspoons Dijon mustard
¼ cup jarred diced pimiento, drained well
3 tablespoons thinly sliced green onion
¼ cup mayonnaise
¼ teaspoon salt

TOPPING
2 tablespoons diced pimiento
2 tablespoons shredded sharp Cheddar cheese

Halve the eggs lengthwise, transfer the yolks to a small bowl, and reserve. Set the egg white halves on a platter, cover, and refrigerate.

In a mixing bowl, combine the Cheddar cheese, cream cheese, garlic, jalapeño, Worcestershire sauce, and mustard. Using an electric mixer with a whip attachment, mix until well incorporated, about 2 minutes. Then add the pimiento and green onion, and mix until incorporated. Add the reserved egg yolks, mayonnaise, and salt, and whip on high speed until well combined. Taste and season accordingly.

Spoon the mixture into a pastry bag fitted with a plain or large star tip, then pipe the mixture evenly into the egg white halves. Or fill the eggs with a spoon, dividing the filling evenly. Top each egg half with ¼ teaspoon of pimiento and ¼ teaspoon of cheese.

CHILAQUILE DEVILED EGGS

Makes 24

This recipe was inspired by chilaquiles, a traditional Mexican dish made with crispy tortilla chips and salsa simmered together, and often topped with an egg. Serve them with an assortment of Mexican beers at your next fiesta.

1 dozen hard-cooked eggs (page 25)

FILLING
½ cup crushed tortilla chips
6 tablespoons salsa verde
¼ cup mayonnaise
¼ cup sour cream
1 teaspoon minced pickled jalapeños
1 tablespoon finely chopped fresh cilantro
¼ teaspoon salt

TOPPING
⅓ cup shredded pepper Jack cheese
⅓ cup crushed tortilla chips

Halve the eggs lengthwise and transfer the yolks to a mixing bowl. Set the egg white halves on a platter, cover, and refrigerate.

In a small bowl, combine the tortilla chips and salsa to soak for 5 minutes.

Meanwhile, with a fork, mash the yolks to a smooth consistency. Add the mayonnaise, sour cream, jalapeños, cilantro, and salt, and mix until smooth. (You can also do this using an electric mixer with a whip attachment.) Stir in the soaked chips and salsa, and mix until well combined. Taste and season accordingly.

Spoon the mixture into a pastry bag fitted with a large plain tip, then pipe the mixture evenly into the egg white halves. Or fill the eggs with a spoon, dividing the filling evenly.

To make the topping, in a small bowl, mix together the cheese and chips. Top each egg half with about 1 heaping teaspoon of the mixture.

INDIAN CURRY DEVILED EGGS

Makes 24

Eggs can be a blank canvas on which you can experiment with adding an exotic accent. In this recipe, I called on the rich, intricate curry spices of India to bring a vibrant flavor to the eggs. Currants lend a hint of sweetness to the filling, and a topping of mango chutney adds a zippy contrast.

1 dozen hard-cooked eggs (page 25)

FILLING

3 tablespoons mayonnaise
3 tablespoons plain yogurt
¼ to ½ teaspoon Tabasco sauce
2 teaspoons curry powder
¼ to ½ teaspoon salt
2 tablespoons dried currants
2 tablespoons minced celery

TOPPING

2 tablespoons mango chutney (see Tip)
24 small fresh parsley leaves

Halve the eggs lengthwise and transfer the yolks to a mixing bowl. Set the egg white halves on a platter, cover, and refrigerate.

With a fork, mash the yolks to a smooth consistency. Add the mayonnaise, yogurt, Tabasco sauce, curry powder, and salt, and mix until smooth. (You can also do this using an electric mixer with a whip attachment.) Stir in the currants and celery. Taste and season accordingly.

Spoon the mixture into a pastry bag fitted with a large plain tip, then pipe the mixture evenly into the egg white halves. Or fill the eggs with a spoon, dividing the filling evenly. Top each egg half with a heaping ¼ teaspoon of chutney and a parsley leaf.

TAHINI & TABBOULEH DEVILED EGGS

Makes 24

These eggs get their delicious appeal from creamy sesame tahini. If you like a little heat, add a pinch of cayenne pepper to the filling. The recipe uses homemade tabbouleh, but you can always pick up some from your grocer's deli if you're pressed for time.

1 dozen hard-cooked eggs (page 25)

FILLING
¼ cup mayonnaise
¼ cup plain yogurt
2 tablespoons tahini
1 teaspoon minced fresh garlic
2 teaspoons fresh lemon juice
¼ teaspoon salt

TOPPING
¾ cup Tabbouleh (recipe follows)

Halve the eggs lengthwise and transfer the yolks to a mixing bowl. Set the egg white halves on a platter, cover, and refrigerate.

With a fork, mash the yolks to a smooth consistency. Add the mayonnaise, yogurt, tahini, garlic, lemon juice, and salt, and mix until smooth. (You can also do this using an electric mixer with a whip attachment.)

Spoon the mixture into a pastry bag fitted with a plain or large star tip, then pipe the mixture evenly into the egg white halves. Or fill the eggs with a spoon, dividing the filling evenly. Taste and season accordingly.

Top each egg half with about ½ tablespoon of the tabbouleh, or press each egg into the mixture to do a fun coating.

TABBOULEH
Makes ¾ cup

3 tablespoons dried bulgur wheat
⅛ teaspoon salt
3 tablespoons boiling water
1 tablespoon fresh lemon juice
1 teaspoon olive oil
2 tablespoons small-diced tomato
3 tablespoons chopped fresh parsley

In a heatproof measuring cup, combine the bulgur and salt, add the boiling water, and quickly cover with plastic wrap. Let sit for 1 hour, or until all the water is absorbed and the bulgur is tender. Stir in the remaining ingredients. Refrigerate until ready to use.

FENNEL, ORANGE & HARISSA DEVILED EGGS

Makes 24

Fennel has a distinctive, refreshing anise flavor, the intensity of which varies between its fronds, bulb, and seeds. In this recipe, I used all three to enhance its licorice notes, which pair wonderfully with tart-sweet citrus. A dash of vibrant red harissa on top adds a colorful and spicy contrast.

1 dozen hard-cooked eggs (page 25)

FILLING
4 tablespoons mayonnaise
2 tablespoons sour cream
1½ teaspoons harissa (see Tip)
2 tablespoons fresh orange juice
1½ teaspoons orange zest
1 teaspoon toasted, well-crushed fennel seeds (see page 33)
¼ teaspoon salt

TOPPING
1 teaspoon fresh orange juice
½ teaspoon extra-virgin olive oil
⅓ cup very tiny-diced fresh fennel bulb
1 tablespoon chopped fresh fennel fronds
1 to 2 tablespoons harissa
2 teaspoons orange zest

Halve the eggs lengthwise and transfer the yolks to a mixing bowl. Set the egg white halves on a platter, cover, and refrigerate.

With a fork, mash the yolks to a smooth consistency. Add the mayonnaise, sour cream, harissa, orange juice, orange zest, fennel seeds, and salt, and mix until smooth. (You can also do this using an electric mixer with a whip attachment.) Taste and season accordingly.

Spoon the mixture into a pastry bag fitted with a plain or large star tip, then pipe the mixture evenly into the egg white halves. Or fill the eggs with a spoon, dividing the filling evenly.

To make the topping, in a small bowl, mix together the orange juice, olive oil, fennel bulb, and fennel fronds. Top each egg half with ⅛ to ¼ teaspoon of harissa, depending upon how spicy you like it, and then about ½ teaspoon of the fennel mixture and a sprinkle of orange zest.

TWO-BITE "CARBONARA" DEVILED DUCK EGGS

Makes 12

A playful take on the classic pasta dish, all done up in a rich duck egg. If you have fresh peas growing in your yard, then by all means use them—just give them a quick blanch. Garnish with tender, delicate little pea vine shoots.

6 hard-cooked duck eggs (page 25)

FILLING
⅓ cup chopped pancetta (about 2 ounces)
⅓ cup frozen petit peas, defrosted, or blanched fresh peas
2 tablespoons mayonnaise
3 tablespoons heavy cream
1½ teaspoons Dijon mustard
¼ teaspoon salt

TOPPING
2 tablespoons grated high-quality parmesan cheese, such as
    Parmigiano-Reggiano
24 tiny pea vine shoots or peas
Freshly ground black pepper

Halve the eggs lengthwise, transfer the yolks to a mixing bowl, and reserve. Set the egg white halves on a platter, cover, and refrigerate.

In a small frying pan, cook the pancetta over medium heat until crispy, 3 to 5 minutes. Drain well.

Place the peas in a small bowl and mash with a large spoon or fork.

With a fork, mash the yolks to a smooth consistency. Add the mashed peas, mayonnaise, cream, mustard, and salt, and mix until smooth. (You can also do this using an electric mixer with a whip attachment.) Stir in the pancetta. Taste and season accordingly.

Spoon the mixture into a small pastry bag fitted with a plain tip, then pipe the mixture evenly into the egg white halves. Or fill the eggs with a spoon, dividing the filling evenly. Top each egg half with a sprinkle of cheese, a pea vine shoot, and a grind of pepper.

DEVILED QUAIL EGGS & CAVIAR

Makes 24

Delicate quail eggs add instant glamour to any cocktail party. These are a sophisticated little bite to pair with a dollop of caviar and a festive glass of bubbly. There are many different varieties of caviar available today that can fit any budget.

1 dozen hard-cooked quail eggs (page 25)

FILLING
2 tablespoons crème fraîche
1 teaspoon mayonnaise
⅛ teaspoon salt

TOPPING
1 tablespoon crème fraîche
¼ teaspoon fresh lemon juice
2 tablespoons caviar
24 very thin lengthwise slices fresh chives

Halve the eggs lengthwise and transfer the yolks to a mixing bowl. Set the egg white halves on a platter, cover, and refrigerate.

With a fork, mash the yolks to a smooth consistency. Add the crème fraîche, mayonnaise, and salt, and mix until smooth. Taste and season accordingly.

Spoon the mixture into a small pastry bag fitted with a tiny plain or star tip, then pipe the mixture evenly into the egg white halves. Or fill the eggs with a spoon, dividing the filling evenly.

To make the topping, combine the crème fraîche and lemon juice in a tiny bowl. Top each egg half with ⅛ teaspoon of the crème fraîche mixture, ¼ teaspoon of caviar, and a slice of chive.

❧ TIP ❧

Crème fraîche can be either purchased or made at home. See page 33 for the recipe. Edible gold flakes can be substituted for the crème fraîche as an elegant accent.

LOBSTER DEVILED EGGS

Makes 24

Lobster in butter, a luxurious combination, was the inspiration for these gourmet eggs. White wine-poached lobster is added to the lush filling, which has butter whipped into it. Ooh-la-la! Be sure to read the recipe all the way through and remember to save your lobster poaching liquid for use in the filling.

1 dozen hard-cooked eggs (page 25)

FILLING
4 tablespoons salted butter, softened
3 tablespoons mayonnaise
¾ teaspoon country Dijon mustard
¼ teaspoon salt
¼ cup reserved lobster poaching liquid, cooled
½ cup Wine-Poached Lobster (recipe follows)

TOPPING
¼ cup Wine-Poached Lobster (recipe follows)
1 teaspoon fresh lemon juice
1 teaspoon lemon zest
1 teaspoon extra-virgin olive oil
1 tablespoon thinly sliced fresh chives

Halve the eggs lengthwise and transfer the yolks to a mixing bowl. Set the egg white halves on a platter, cover, and refrigerate.

In a mixing bowl with a whip attachment, whip together the yolks and butter until smooth. Add the mayonnaise, mustard, and salt, and mix until smooth. Add the lobster poaching liquid and mix until smooth. Stir in the lobster. Taste and season accordingly.

Spoon the mixture into a pastry bag fitted with a large plain tip, then pipe the mixture evenly into the egg white halves. Or fill the eggs with a spoon, dividing the filling evenly.

To make the topping, in a small bowl, mix together the lobster, lemon juice, lemon zest, olive oil, and chives. Top each egg half with about ½ teaspoon of the mixture.

WINE-POACHED LOBSTER

Makes ¾ cup, enough for 1 recipe

2 tablespoons butter
½ cup dry white wine
6 to 7 ounces raw lobster meat, cut into 1- to 2-inch pieces (about ¾ cup)

In a small saucepan, heat the butter and white wine over medium heat. When the mixture comes to a light simmer, add the lobster, stir, and cook, covered, for 3 to 4 minutes, or until opaque and just cooked through. Remove the lobster from the cooking liquid with a slotted spoon (reserve the cooking liquid) and finely chop the cooked lobster.

❖ TIP ❖

Fresh langoustine or slipper lobster meat can be a less expensive alternative to lobster tail. An 8-ounce lobster tail in the shell yields 6 to 7 ounces of raw meat.

LUXE TRUFFLE DEVILED EGGS

Makes 20

Everyone needs one quick, easy, go-to recipe that looks and tastes like a million bucks. These eggs work like a charm: the fragrant truffle oil adds rich, sexy appeal, and a sprinkle of black lava salt lends an elegant finish. Make them super bling by adding a tiny flake of edible 24k gold leaf to each.

1 dozen hard-cooked eggs (page 25)

FILLING
2 tablespoons mayonnaise
2 tablespoons sour cream or crème fraîche
2 tablespoons truffle oil
¼ teaspoon salt

TOPPING
Black lava salt
Fresh-cracked black pepper
20 tiny chive flowers (optional)

Halve the eggs lengthwise and transfer the yolks to a mixing bowl. Set 20 egg white halves on a platter, cover, and refrigerate. This recipe uses 12 egg yolks, but only yields enough filling for 20 halves; reserve the extra 4 whites for another use.

With a fork, mash the yolks to a smooth consistency. Add the mayonnaise, sour cream, truffle oil, and salt, and mix until smooth. (You can also do this using an electric mixer with a whip attachment.) Taste and season accordingly.

Spoon the mixture into a pastry bag fitted with a plain or large star tip, then pipe the mixture evenly into the egg white halves. Or fill the eggs with a spoon, dividing the filling evenly.

Top each egg half with a tiny sprinkle of black lava salt, a grind of fresh-cracked black pepper, and a chive flower, if using.

❖ TIP ❖

Specialty salts, such as black lava salt or other gourmet varieties, are available both online and in specialty and gourmet food stores.

DEVILED EGGS DUXELLES

Makes 24

I just love mushrooms, so the opportunity to put them in deviled eggs was irresistible. The mushrooms are finely chopped and cooked down for intensity. If wild mushrooms are available at your local farmers' market, they would be a delicious alternative to standard varieties. The thyme leaves sprinkled on top give this earthy offering a fragrant finish.

1 dozen hard-cooked eggs (page 25)

FILLING
6 tablespoons mayonnaise
1½ teaspoons Dijon mustard
1 teaspoon Worcestershire sauce
¼ teaspoon salt
½ teaspoon finely minced fresh thyme
½ cup Mushroom Duxelles (recipe follows)

TOPPING
¼ cup Mushroom Duxelles (recipe follows)
24 very tiny fresh thyme sprigs

Halve the eggs lengthwise and transfer the yolks to a mixing bowl. Set the egg white halves on a platter, cover, and refrigerate.

With a fork, mash the yolks to a smooth consistency. Add the mayonnaise, mustard, Worcestershire sauce, and salt, and mix until smooth. (You can also do this using an electric mixer with a whip attachment.) Stir in the thyme and duxelles. Taste and season accordingly.

Spoon the mixture into a pastry bag fitted with a plain or large star tip, then pipe the mixture evenly into the egg white halves. Or fill the eggs with a spoon, dividing the filling evenly. Top each egg half with about ½ teaspoon of duxelles and a sprig of thyme.

MUSHROOM DUXELLES

Makes about ¾ cup, enough for 1 recipe

2 cups coarsely chopped white or cremini mushrooms
1 tablespoon butter
2 tablespoons minced shallot
1 tablespoon minced fresh garlic
2 tablespoons dry sherry

In a food processor, pulse the mushrooms until finely chopped. (If you don't have a food processor, then chop very finely by hand.) Heat a 10-inch nonstick sauté pan over medium heat. Add the butter and let melt. Add the shallot and garlic, and cook for 1 to 2 minutes, until soft but not browned. Then add the mushrooms, and cook until the pan is almost dry and the mushrooms have reduced. Add the sherry and cook down until dry, 3 to 4 more minutes. Remove from the heat and let cool.

❖ TIP ❖

I like to use half button or cremini mushrooms and half wild mushrooms, such as morel, porcini, or chanterelle, when in season.

EMERALD ASPARAGUS & SWEET ONION DEVILED EGGS

Makes 24

Fresh, brilliant asparagus and sweet white onions, such as Vidalia, Walla Walla, or Texas Sweets, pair up to showcase the garden's seasonal bounty in these emerald gems.

1 dozen hard-cooked eggs (page 25)

FILLING
12 spears baby asparagus, bottoms trimmed
3 tablespoons mayonnaise
3 tablespoons sour cream
1 teaspoon fresh lemon juice
½ teaspoon salt
1 teaspoon finely minced fresh mint
2 tablespoons minced sweet white onion

TOPPING
24 reserved, halved asparagus tips

In a medium pot, bring 4 cups of water to a boil, then add the asparagus and quickly blanch for 30 seconds. Immediately remove the asparagus from the boiling water and run under cold water to stop the cooking. Drain well. Cut off the tips, slice the tips in half lengthwise, and reserve for garnish. Slice the stems (you should have about ½ cup) and puree in a food processor with the mayonnaise, sour cream, lemon juice, and salt, until smooth.

Halve the eggs lengthwise and transfer the yolks to a mixing bowl. Set the egg white halves on a platter, cover, and refrigerate.

With a fork, mash the yolks to a smooth consistency. Add the puréed asparagus mixture, and mix until smooth. (You can also do this using an electric mixer with a whip attachment.) Stir in the mint and onion. Taste and season accordingly. Spoon the mixture into a pastry bag fitted with a plain or large star tip, then pipe the mixture evenly into the egg white halves. Or fill the eggs with a spoon, dividing the filling evenly. Top each egg half with a piece of asparagus.

❖ TIP ❖

*For a polka dot effect, firmly pack the
eggs into a narrow container so that
they are all touching, and do not stir
them. The eggs will be lighter pink
or white where they touch, lending a
perky polka dot pattern.*

BEET'ING HEART DEVILED EGGS

Makes 24

*I'm all for an appetizer that doubles as a fun craft project, and these eggs
certainly fit the bill. Pickled beet juice turns the whites deep pink and makes
these ideal for serving up on Valentine's Day or Easter. Kids will love helping.*

1 (15-ounce) can sliced pickled beets
½ cup red wine vinegar
¼ cup sugar
1 dozen hard-cooked eggs (page 25)

FILLING
3 tablespoons mayonnaise
3 tablespoons sour cream
2 tablespoons stone-ground mustard
2 tablespoons minced red onion
¼ teaspoon sugar
¼ teaspoon salt
Fresh-cracked black pepper

TOPPING
¼ cup reserved small-diced pickled beets, drained well
2 tablespoons thinly sliced green onion

To pickle the eggs, drain the beet liquid into a deep medium container and
reserve the beets separately. Add the red wine vinegar and sugar to the beet
liquid and stir to dissolve the sugar. Peel the hard-cooked eggs and add to
the mixture, being sure they are submerged. Cover and let sit for about 4
hours, refrigerated. Stir often to color evenly. Drain the eggs well, pat dry
on paper towels, and discard the beet liquid. Halve the eggs lengthwise and
transfer the yolks to a mixing bowl. Set the egg white halves on a platter,
cover, and refrigerate.

To finish the eggs, with a fork, mash the yolks to a smooth consistency. Add
the mayonnaise, sour cream, mustard, red onion, sugar, and salt, and mix
until smooth. (You can also do this using an electric mixer with a whip
attachment.) Add salt and black pepper to taste.

Spoon the mixture into a pastry bag fitted with a plain or large star tip,
then pipe the mixture evenly into the egg white halves. Or fill the eggs with
a spoon, dividing the filling evenly. Top each egg half with ½ teaspoon of
pickled beets and a sprinkle of green onion.

❧ TIP ❧

*To make chipotle chile puree,
place canned chipotle peppers in
adobo sauce, with the sauce, in
a food processor or blender and
puree until smooth. Freeze any
extra puree for another use.*

CHIPOTLE DEVILED EGGS

Makes 24

I've been making these for years and they have become a cocktail-party staple. The spicy tomato topping adds textural and visual pizzazz. Serve these with a refreshing margarita for a festive pairing.

1 dozen hard-cooked eggs (page 25)

FILLING

3 tablespoons mayonnaise
3 tablespoons regular or low-fat sour cream
½ teaspoon Dijon mustard
1 to 2 tablespoons chipotle chile puree (see Tip)
1 teaspoon minced fresh garlic
¼ teaspoon salt
2 tablespoons thinly sliced green onion

TOPPING

½ cup small-diced tomatoes
1 tablespoon minced white onion
2 tablespoons chopped fresh cilantro
1 to 2 teaspoons chipotle chile puree

Halve the eggs lengthwise and transfer the yolks to a mixing bowl. Set the egg white halves on a platter, cover, and refrigerate.

With a fork, mash the yolks to a smooth consistency. Add the mayonnaise, sour cream, mustard, chipotle puree, garlic, and salt, and mix until smooth. (You can also do this using an electric mixer with a whip attachment.) Stir in the green onion. Taste and season accordingly.

Spoon the mixture into a pastry bag fitted with a plain or large star tip, then pipe the mixture evenly into the egg white halves. Or fill the eggs with a spoon, dividing the filling evenly.

To make the topping, in a small bowl, mix together the tomatoes, onion, cilantro, and chipotle puree. Top each egg half with about 1 teaspoon of the topping.

CRAB LOUIS DEVILED EGGS

Makes 24

The iconic salad is the basis for these tempting stuffed eggs. Serve them on their own, or for a double whammy, as the garnish for a Crab Louis salad. This recipe can be made with either canned or fresh crab; if you choose to use fresh crab, be sure to save the really pretty pieces for the topping.

1 dozen hard-cooked eggs (page 25)

FILLING
2 tablespoons mayonnaise
4 tablespoons tomato chili sauce
2 tablespoons sweet pickle relish
1 teaspoon Worcestershire sauce
¼ teaspoon salt
½ cup crabmeat, well drained

TOPPING
3 tablespoons small-diced tomato
3 tablespoons small-diced black olive
¼ cup crabmeat, well drained

Halve the eggs lengthwise and transfer the yolks to a mixing bowl. Set the egg white halves on a platter, cover, and refrigerate.

With a fork, mash the yolks to a smooth consistency. Add the mayonnaise, chili sauce, relish, Worcestershire sauce, and salt, and mix until smooth. (You can also do this using an electric mixer with a whip attachment.) Stir in the crabmeat. Taste and season accordingly.

Spoon the mixture into a pastry bag fitted with a large plain tip, then pipe the mixture evenly into the egg white halves. Or fill the eggs with a spoon, dividing the filling evenly.

Top each egg half with a little tomato, olive, and crabmeat.

CAESAR SALAD DEVILED EGGS

Makes 24

All the components of the perennially popular salad are mingled in this innovative stuffed egg, including the often overlooked anchovy. If you are an anchovy lover like I am, top each egg with the Cadillac of them all, a Spanish marinated white anchovy.

1 dozen hard-cooked eggs (page 25)

FILLING

6 tablespoons mayonnaise
1 tablespoon Dijon mustard
1 teaspoon fresh lemon juice
1 tablespoon Worcestershire sauce
1 teaspoon anchovy paste or finely minced anchovy
1 teaspoon lemon zest
2 teaspoons minced fresh garlic
2 tablespoons grated Parmesan cheese
½ teaspoon freshly ground black pepper

TOPPING

¼ cup thinly sliced hearts of romaine lettuce
24 small pieces anchovy fillet (optional)

Halve the eggs lengthwise and transfer the yolks to a mixing bowl. Set the egg white halves on a platter, cover, and refrigerate.

With a fork, mash the yolks to a smooth consistency. Add the mayonnaise, mustard, lemon juice, Worcestershire sauce, anchovy paste, lemon zest, garlic, Parmesan, and pepper, and mix until smooth. (You can also do this using an electric mixer with a whip attachment.) Taste and season accordingly.

Spoon the mixture into a pastry bag fitted with a plain or large star tip, then pipe the mixture evenly into the egg white halves. Or fill the eggs with a spoon, dividing the filling evenly.

Top each egg half with a small pouf of lettuce and a piece of anchovy fillet, if desired.

❧ TIP ❧

For even more zesty pop, toss the lettuce in a squeeze of fresh lemon and grate some high-quality Parmesan over the top.

RADISHES & BUTTER DEVILED EGGS

Makes 20

Elegant in their simplicity, springtime radishes swiped in butter and sprinkled with sea salt are a quintessential French appetizer and were the inspiration for this lovely rendition of deviled eggs. With their artful flourish of radish "flowers," these eggs are a fantastic opportunity to practice your garnishing techniques; rainbow radishes give a lovely splash of color if you can find them at the market.

1 dozen hard-cooked eggs (page 25)

FILLING
4 tablespoons salted butter, softened
2 tablespoons mayonnaise
1½ teaspoons stone-ground mustard
¼ teaspoon salt

TOPPING
40 thinly shaved slices radish
20 tiny sprigs fresh dill
Coarse sea salt
Fresh-cracked black pepper

Halve the eggs lengthwise and transfer the yolks to a mixing bowl. Set 20 egg whites halves on a platter, cover, and refrigerate. This recipe uses 12 egg yolks, but only yields enough filling for 20 halves; reserve the extra 4 whites for another use.

Using a mixer with a whip attachment, whip together the yolks and butter until smooth. Add the mayonnaise, mustard, and salt, and mix until smooth. Taste and season accordingly.

Spoon the mixture into a pastry bag fitted with a plain or large star tip, then pipe the mixture evenly into the egg white halves. Or fill the eggs with a spoon, dividing the filling evenly.

Make a small cut one-third of the way through each radish slice. Fit 2 slices together at the slits to make a "flower." Top each egg half with 1 radish flower and a sprig of dill. Sprinkle lightly with coarse sea salt and fresh-cracked black pepper.

SUNNY ROASTED RED PEPPER DEVILED EGGS

Makes 24

These eggs are like a little bite of Spanish sunshine; sweet roasted red peppers, a hint of smoky paprika, and a cheery hit of orange are reminiscent of the classic romesco sauce, especially topped with toasted sliced almonds. If roasted red pepper pesto is not available, sun-dried tomato pesto is an excellent alternative.

1 dozen hard-cooked eggs (page 25)

FILLING
¼ cup roasted red pepper pesto or sun-dried tomato pesto
¼ cup mayonnaise
1 teaspoon Dijon mustard
2 tablespoons fresh orange juice
1 teaspoon finely minced orange zest
1½ teaspoons smoked paprika
¼ teaspoon red pepper flakes
Salt

TOPPING
2 tablespoons toasted sliced almonds
Smoked paprika

Halve the eggs lengthwise and transfer the yolks to a mixing bowl. Set the egg white halves on a platter, cover, and refrigerate.

With a fork, mash the yolks to a smooth consistency. Add the pesto, mayonnaise, mustard, orange juice, orange zest, smoked paprika, and red pepper flakes, and mix until smooth. (You can also do this using an electric mixer with a whip attachment.) Taste the egg mixture and add a little salt if needed; pestos differ in salt content.

Spoon the mixture into a pastry bag fitted with a plain or large star tip, then pipe the mixture evenly into the egg white halves. Or fill the eggs with a spoon, dividing the filling evenly.

Top each egg half with a sprinkle of almonds and dust lightly with the smoked paprika.

PUMPKIN PIE DEVILED EGGS

Makes 24

This Thanksgiving, while everyone is scrambling to make pumpkin pie for their holiday gathering, you'll be the talk of the table when you show up with this inspired holiday appetizer. The eggs are soaked in sweet cinnamon nutmeg syrup, stuffed with a savory spiced-pumpkin filling, and topped off with salted, candied pecans. Be sure to read through the recipe completely before beginning.

1 dozen hard-cooked eggs (page 25)
1 recipe Cinnamon Nutmeg Syrup (recipe follows)

FILLING
6 tablespoons canned pure pumpkin
2 tablespoons sour cream
1 tablespoon honey
¼ teaspoon ground nutmeg
¼ teaspoon ground cinnamon
½ teaspoon salt
2 tablespoons mayonnaise

TOPPING
½ cup Candied Pecans (recipe follows)
1 tablespoon Cinnamon Nutmeg Syrup (recipe follows)

Place the peeled hard-cooked eggs into a deep vessel. Reserve 1 tablespoon of the Cinnamon Nutmeg Syrup for the topping, and pour the remaining syrup over the eggs. Cover and let soak, refrigerated, for 2 to 3 hours. (Don't soak for more than 4 hours, or the eggs will become hard.)

Remove the eggs from the syrup, and pat dry with paper towels. Halve the eggs lengthwise and transfer the yolks to a mixing bowl. Set the egg white halves on a platter, cover, and refrigerate.

In a small bowl, combine the pumpkin, sour cream, honey, spices, and salt. »

With a fork, mash the yolks to a smooth consistency and mix in the mayonnaise. Then add the pumpkin mixture, and mix until smooth. (You can also do this using an electric mixer with a whip attachment.)

Spoon the mixture into a small pastry bag fitted with a plain tip, then pipe the mixture evenly into the egg white halves. Or fill the eggs with a spoon, dividing the filling evenly. Top each egg half with a few candied pecans and drizzle with ½ teaspoon of the reserved syrup.

CINNAMON NUTMEG SYRUP
Makes about 3 cups

1 cup water
2 cups sugar
¼ teaspoon ground cinnamon
¼ teaspoon ground nutmeg

Combine all of the ingredients in a small saucepan and bring to a boil. Remove from the heat and let cool. Store refrigerated until ready to use.

CANDIED PECANS
Save extra nuts for snacking!
Makes ¾ cup

1½ teaspoons butter, melted
2 tablespoons honey
⅛ teaspoon ground nutmeg
⅛ teaspoon ground cinnamon
¼ teaspoon salt
½ cup coarsely chopped pecans

Combine all of the ingredients in a small nonstick skillet and toss well to coat. Cook over medium heat until the nuts are lightly browned and caramelized, 3 to 5 minutes. Remove from the heat and spread out on a baking sheet. Let cool completely.

LARGE-BATCH DEVILED EGGS RECIPE TEMPLATE

Makes 72

Designed for large events or catering. This recipe uses a different cooking method and also has a little butter whipped into the filling, which helps make it firm when chilled and decreases the risk of "unfortunate filling issues" during transportation. The filling recipe is a nicely seasoned base for you to put your personal spin on.

36 large chicken eggs

SEASONED DEVILED-EGG BASE
4 tablespoons salted butter, softened
¾ cup mayonnaise
1 tablespoon Dijon mustard
½ teaspoon hot sauce
1½ teaspoons Worcestershire sauce
¾ teaspoon salt

ADD-INS
2 tablespoons finely minced white onion
¼ cup finely minced celery
¼ cup thinly sliced green onion

Place the eggs in an 8-quart nonreactive saucepan, and add cold water to 3 inches above the eggs. Bring to a boil over medium-high heat. As soon as the eggs come to a boil, decrease the heat to a very low simmer and immediately set a timer for 10 minutes. (Be sure to watch while the eggs come to a boil, to be ready to immediately decrease the heat and start timing.)

After the timer goes off, quickly remove the pan of eggs from the heat and place in the sink. Add 4 cups of ice to the pan and run cold water over the eggs until they are cooled. When the eggs are thoroughly cooled, refrigerate for up to 5 days or carefully peel them under running water. »

When you are ready to stuff the eggs, halve them lengthwise and transfer the yolks to a mixing bowl. Set the egg white halves on a large platter or in glass baking dishes, cover, and refrigerate.

Using an electric mixer fitted with a whip attachment, start mixing the egg yolks on medium-low speed for 1 minute. Add the butter and mix for an additional 2 minutes, or until smooth. Then add the mayonnaise, mustard, hot sauce, Worcestershire sauce, and salt. Mix for another minute, or until very smooth, scraping down the sides of the mixer occasionally.

Once you have a nicely seasoned deviled-egg base, you can mix in some basics, such as the white onion, celery, and green onion.

From this point you can add in and customize your deviled eggs. Get inspired with some of the following:

Bacon, crumbled
Cheeses, grated or crumbled
Chili powder
Cucumber, minced
Curry powder
Fresh herbs, minced
Nuts, toasted
Olives, chopped
Salami, minced
Shrimp or crab
Sun-dried tomatoes, minced
Sweet pickle relish

To fill your eggs, fill a pastry bag fitted with a large plain tip or large star tip, then pipe the mixture evenly into the egg white halves. Garnish as desired. Be sure to refrigerate well before transporting so the filling gets firm.

So get creative—the Deviled Egg possibilities are endless . . .

METRIC EQUIVALENTS & CONVERSIONS

METRIC CONVERSION FORMULAS

Ounces to grams	Ounces by 28.35
Pounds to kilograms	Pounds by 0.454
Teaspoons to milliliters	Teaspoons by 4.93
Tablespoons to milliliters	Tablespoons by 14.79
Fluid ounces to milliliters	Fluid ounces by 29.57
Cups to milliliters	Cups by 236.59
Cups to liters	Cups by 0.236
Pints to liters	Pints by 0.473
Quarts to liters	Quarts by 0.946
Inches to centimeters	Inches by 2.54

APPROXIMATE METRIC EQUIVALENTS

VOLUME

¼ teaspoon	1 milliliter
½ teaspoon	2.5 milliliters
¾ teaspoon	4 milliliters
1 teaspoon	5 milliliters
1½ teaspoons	7.5 milliliters
1 tablespoon (½ fluid ounce)	15 milliliters
2 tablespoons (1 fluid ounce)	30 milliliters
¼ cup	60 milliliters
⅓ cup	80 milliliters
½ cup (4 fluid ounces)	120 milliliters
¾ cup	180 milliliters
1 cup (8 fluid ounces)	240 milliliters
2 cups (1 pint)	460 milliliters
4 cups (1 quart)	0.95 liter
1 quart plus ¼ cup	1 liter
4 quarts (1 gallon)	3.8 liters

WEIGHT

¼ ounce	7 grams
½ ounce	14 grams
¾ ounce	21 grams
1 ounce	28 grams
2 ounces	57 grams
3 ounces	85 grams
4 ounces (¼ pound)	113 grams
8 ounces (½ pound)	227 grams
16 ounces (1 pound)	454 grams

LENGTH

⅛ inch	3 millimeters
¼ inch	6 millimeters
½ inch	1.23 centimeters
1 inch	2.5 centimeters
2 inches	5 centimeters
2½ inches	6 centimeters
4 inches	10 centimeters

Information compiled from a variety of sources, including *Recipes into Type* by Joan Whitman and Dolores Simon (Newton, MA: Biscuit Books, 2000); *The New Food Lover's Companion* by Sharon Tyler Herbst (Hauppauge, NY: Barron's, 1995); and *Rosemary Brown's Big Kitchen Instruction Book* (Kansas City, MO: Andrews McMeel, 1998).

METRIC EQUIVALENTS & CONVERSIONS

INDEX